SERGING AUSTRALIA

OVERLOCKER ARTISTRY

Dear Niva

Many Happy Stitches!

Regards

Anne

Nov 2004

By Anne van der Kley

sergi

25 Izett Street Prahran Victoria 3181 Australia
Tel: 6 13 9529 4400 Fax: 6 13 9525 1172

Email: penguin@netspace.net.au
Website: http://www.penguin-threads.com.au

Serging Australia by Anne van der Kley

Photographer: Andre Martin 02 9417 7286
Stylist: Kathy Tripp 02 9968 4063

Printed by Altshul Printers
239 Separation St Northcote Vic 3070 Australia

Published by:

AUSSIE
PUBLISHERS

about serging Australia

Please don't get too upset as an Australian that I refer to a serger throughout this book, rather than as an overlocker: the term is a familiar one to any sewer. The reason is based in pure practicality; I am a pathetically slow typist and dreadfully inaccurate. The overlocker was either an oberlocker, overlicker, or an oberlicker; the worst I did with serger was serfer.

I am only pleased that a computer allows easy righting of spelling wrongs, or I would probably have needed treatment for solvent abuse with the amount of fumes wafting about with all the correction fluid I needed. I'll rationalize it by saying that as you serge, an overlock stitch is formed. It's quicker to type.

Serging Australia contains many different creations. I have used some poetic license in the names given to the projects, trying to keep a truly Australian theme. I have introduced my creations in letters to a friend in the USA and have made out that I have moved to the country. I am very fortunate that I know 2 great women with the same initials, J.F.; they are unrelated but share the surname. One, Janice, does indeed live in the USA, the other, Julie, in the Blue Mountains, west of Sydney where I am also fortunate enough to live. They both share a passion for sewing and a great generosity of spirit and a huge sense of fun. Share J.F.'s letters from me.

I set myself 2 objectives: serger projects that would be unexpected, flouting traditions and stereotypes, and projects that required no special accessories. I believe that I have achieved both objectives.

I could not make any spelling concessions; I might be a lousy typist but colour is colour not color, even though the spell check fought with me the entire way. This book is about creating, not spelling. I hope Serging Australia – Overlocker Artistry stimulates you to reproduce any of my creations or better still to create your own.

Anne

CONTENTS

S

If all else fails,
follow the instructions...

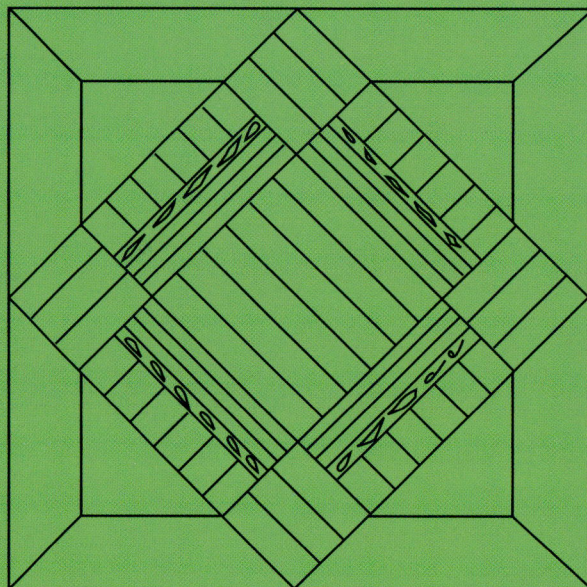

Example designs

technical stuff

Not all sergers are created equal. Far from it. There is a quantum leap in ability and performance between the different ends of the market, often measured in not just how much you use the serger, but also what you use it for. That is not to say there are not some very good sergers in between, there certainly are. For so-called everyday use, usually garment construction, most of the budget sergers perform adequately. Challenge them with extremely heavy or ultra light fabrics, decorative or embroidery threads and they often perform poorly.

If you have the opportunity, buy the very best you can afford. As the price increases so too the ease of threading, all setting adjustments, motor size, speed and the ability to handle a wider variety of fabrics more easily. They usually have more in built features such as memory, looper threaders, visual displays, thread cutters, cover hem, chain stitch, 2-thread conversion. The difference will take you from purely functional serging to overlocker textile art and back again without missing a beat. I liken it to the difference between the cheapest car on the market and a Rolls Royce. They will both take you to your destination, but how easily and comfortably?

The next most important step to enjoying your serger comes down to your dealer and the instruction you receive. A serger, no matter what it cost, is expensive if you do not know how to use it. Ensure your dealer will give reasonable instruction and be equally as responsible by practising steps and techniques as you learn them. It works both ways.

Serging from the baseline

As a nurse, I was always taught that you measured all things from a baseline – temperature, pulse etc. When you knew what the "normal" or "usual" baseline data was, it was easy to work out what was abnormal and unusual. So too with serging. Once you know what setting the baseline is and the usual look of the overlock stitch, you can start playing to create different effects. Most importantly, you also have somewhere to return to.

If you don't understand what the baseline is for your serger, please go and do a basic course with your local dealer: even pay to have them set your serger tensions. A normal "balanced" 4-thread stitch on 2 layers of medium weight even weave fabric, such as homespun, is what you need. Throughout Serging Australia you will find the following tables, with suggested settings. These are all variations from the baseline of a 4 thread balanced stitch of any serger and are general guidelines – for your records and probably your sanity at the serger, write your baseline settings down!

I keep all my serger data as follows:

Left Needle	Right Needle	Upper Looper	Lower Looper
Stitch Length	Differential Feed	Cutting Width	Special

the technical stuff
(cont)

The following table will be used throughout 'Serging Australia'

L.N.	R.N.	U.L.	L.L.
S.L.	D.F.	C.W.	Sp.

Markings or settings on your serger determine how you do your record keeping. It may be marked with a letter, a number, or a lever. Depending upon your machine you may have to access an LCD screen, turn a dial, slide a lever. Some sergers have automatic or pre-set tensioning adjustments. None that I know of automatically adjust the stitch length, differential feed or cutting width, probably because there is no such thing as automatic thread or fabric combinations.

Proper Names

Most serger reference books do not know what brand of serger you own. They don't know if the dials are purple or hot pink. They actually refer to the proper name of the part for uniformity and clarity. Take the time to learn what's what and you will be able to read any reference, any time.

Tension – What is it?

This is not what you should get when you think of sitting at the serger. Only the threads should be tense. The amount of tension on each thread depends upon the stitch you are creating. It also depends upon the thread being in the tension discs properly. Standard threads and a 4 thread balanced stitch give the serger few challenges: tension is at the baseline setting. Start doing a stitch to show off your serger skills and your fancy threads and all of a sudden your tension is all over the place. This is perfectly normal. A serger is a machine and will only do what you tell it to, though I admit, on occasions mine acts like a person with selective deafness. It will only stitch the information it is given and if this is not accurate there is no way it will behave properly.

It is impractical and probably impossible to try and specify adjustments to individual sergers. I have used overall terms to denote changes:

- baseline: your usual or normal setting
- baseline or little looser: a tiny adjustment, a ¼-½ a full number
- looser: around 1 full number less than the baseline
- very loose: at least 2 full numbers less than the baseline
- tighten: at least 2 full numbers higher than the baseline
- neutral (D.F.): both feed dogs moving at the same rate

Needle Reference

The other important measurement is your needle reference point. Most sergers have some markings at the very front of the foot. They are not there to add texture or decoration to the foot, they are actually an indicator of where the needle will enter the fabric to create the seam line – you know, left mark, left needle, right mark, right needle. Important stuff. Refer to the manufacturer's manual for the specifics for your serger. If you can't work this out, the local dealer is the next best reference point.

If you can't thread it, dread it!

This is the best long-cut I know

I believe very strongly that anyone who owns a serger should know how to thread it from scratch. It ultimately saves a lot of anxiety. There is a particular sequence in which a serger is threaded. Refer to your manufacturer's manual for the correct sequence for your model. Unless your serger is a dinosaur, you will usually also find a chart of this sequence inside the front cover that you open to expose the serger's working parts.

Why do you need to know all or any of this? Purely and simply, preventative practice. Serging Australia is about exploring and developing techniques, experimenting with different threads, manipulating textiles and simply playing. There are inherent challenges with this manner of textile artistry – the most common one I experienced was that I was so focused on what I was doing I ran out of thread and actually had to thread completely from scratch.

There is another often overlooked reason – it is impossible to clean your serger properly unless it is completely unthreaded. Brushing and oiling is important and should always be done properly and a whole lot of thread in the way just does not allow this.

Odd numbers

I refer to serging sets of stitches in odd numbers. I do not mean 4 bzillion 393 squillion, rather 1,3,5,etc.

Chaining Off

At the completion of a stitch performed on fabric, the serger continues to run and a thread chain is formed with no fabric under the presser foot.

Serger chain

A chain thread created with no fabric or a water-soluble fabric. Usually made with a combination of decorative threads and varying overlock stitches.

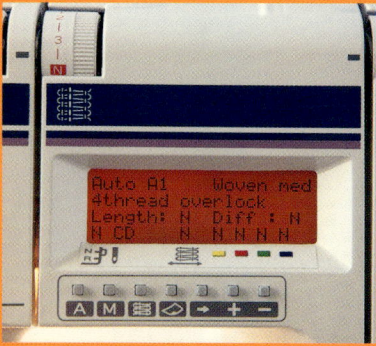

**In-built
instruction book**

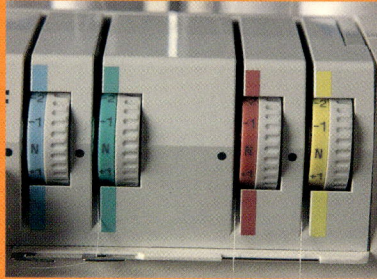

**Colour coded
tension slots**

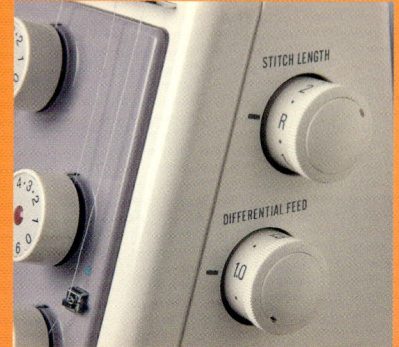

Adjustable dials

**Adjustable
foot pressure**

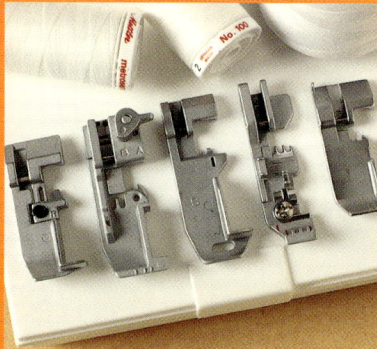

**Standard
presser feet**

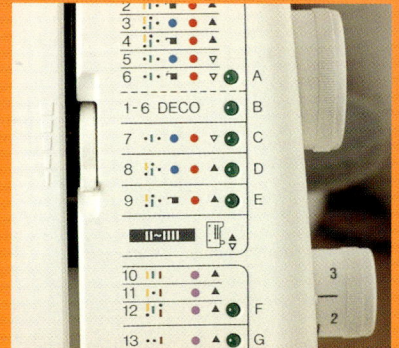

Stitch selector

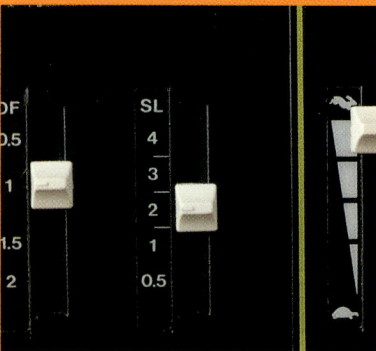

Speed control

the technical stuff
(cont)

How much thread?

Sergers devour thread faster than a teenage football team can empty a fridge of food. It is difficult sometimes to quantify amounts especially when the work is experimental. Just know how to thread from scratch in case of being over zealous.

Flatlocking *and the cutting blade*

Many people will find this personal preference of mine contentious – I NEVER lower my cutting blade to flatlock. I treat the stitch as either a normal 3 thread, cutting off fabric as I go or position my needle with the fabric on the fold and the blade whispering sweet nothings as it passes by. I have seen too many expensive repairs when the blade was not repositioned after flatlocking. It remains your choice. I do suggest that if you lower/disengage your cutting blade, write yourself a note and place it prominently – stuck to your wrist or forehead is good – so you remember to return the blade to its cutting position.

Serging Fine Fabric

Sergers like fine fabrics; they will do a terrific job of stitching them together. They also like to eat them! I have fed my serger too often – you know, right at the beginning of a row when the fabric is not quite under the presser foot, it is chewed up. This is both ugly and expensive. Some simple preventative sergery is the answer – give the feed dogs a snack. A little scrap of fabric or water soluble Avalon®, fed under the presser foot as a `leader` will ensure the fine fabric travels through smoothly. Now the feed dogs have something to sink their teeth into other than your squillion dollar creations.

Imperial or metric?

There is no right answer for this. I know we have been metrified in Australia since the 1960's, I nursed metrically but I do patchwork imperially. I have given both measurements for fabric requirements, but still allude to a ¼ in seam allowance. Convert it as you will, I lost the plot when I had 0.000008mm x 1.233333 mm or something to that effect.

Spelling

The one concession I could not make was spelling; I might be a lousy typist but colour is colour not color. Bear with me.

> *Please use this as a general reference section: nothing will replace a good relationship with your dealer and practicing techniques on your part.*
> *Relax – it is not a tragedy when things don't work out as planned – overlocker artistry is about recycling too.*

Equipment

sergical necessities – equipment

Do yourself a favour and keep a range of good basic equipment and accessories. While many accessories are supplied with your new machine I have found a few extras can make an enormous difference. Please refer to this basic list as a reference – it is handy but by no means exhaustive and you will probably have much of it already.

THREAD – *ALWAYS* use a good quality. If you hold your thread to the light and it looks like mohair, your repairer will love you. It sheds into your tension discs, breaks or disintegrates when you need it most and is a general nuisance. Get rid of it. Cheap thread always ends up becoming the most expensive you can use.

Mettler Metrosene is a standard polyester thread which has a fantastic colour range and can be used on both the serger and sewing machine. Metrocor' and Metrolene' are serger specific and superb threads to use.

Thread quality is even more important when working with machine embroidery threads on a serger. High speed and cheap thread are mutually exclusive. Ensure your thread is colour fast – if there is no indication on the spool don't buy it. Hours spent creating your special item to see it wash down the sink or fade over time is beyond words. The only thing that should fade is the recollection of how long it took to make.

MARKERS – keep a variety on hand. Water-soluble, air erasable, mechanical pencils; the list just keeps on growing. They all have a place with sergers, especially if they take the place of pins.

N.P.I's – 'needle putter inners', otherwise known as needle inserters. Try a couple of different types. They make a big difference to your mental health when you have the right one.

TWEEZERS – a good pair with a precision point are worth their weight in gold, especially when working with fine embroidery threads. Consider buying some from a medical (or should that be sergical?) supplier for the absolute best.

SCISSORS – have a variety on hand, from fine curved decoupage scissors, embroidery and all-purpose scissors to some dressmaking shears.

PINS – try and avoid them near your serger, they can wreck a cutting blade too easily and almost unnoticeably. There are some terrific water soluble alternatives.

NEEDLES – good quality needles are as much an investment as is good thread. They should be replaced at regular intervals, no more than 6 continuous hours of serging. They do a mighty amount of work at very high speed and represent an insignificant cost as part of a garment or in serger artistry.

DENTAL FLOSS THREADER – ever tried to thread the loopers with something a little challenging? No matter how good your looper threaders are, they are not always appropriate. No serger that I know of has a self-threading upper looper, so these little gizmos can be lifesavers.

MEASURING equipment – tape measures, seam gauges patchwork rulers. Have a mixed range on hand; there is no such thing as too many.

CLEANING equipment – brushes of different sizes for the fiddly bits, soft cloths for the outside. A computer vacuum cleaner is handy or use canned air to get even more debris out.

SCREWDRIVERS / ALLEN keys – your serger manual will show which you need. Keep them away from the family and keep a spare somewhere you will remember – in with the chocolates ensures you are reminded periodically.

MISCELLANEOUS – spool net, good quality machine oil, your manufacturer's manual and a good reference text.

Hi J.F.,

Finally time to write. We have had our first major challenge since we 'went bush'. The lovely green country you saw on your last trip seems an eternity ago, replaced by cracked earth, dust, skies bleached of colour, sweltering heat and bushfires.It has been quite terrifying with volunteer Bush Fire Brigades out fighting major outbreaks.

The neighbour's (5 minutes away in the car) little girl said she didn't like the bruised sky - when I looked up, that's exactly what it was - black and blue and bruised looking. So dramatic, all the greenery being swallowed up by orange red flames and leaving clouds of black smoke. I've tried to put it altogether in this 'The Bushfire Quilt' to remember our first year out here.

I think I'll be in the sewers 'Naughty Corner' though ! I pieced it all on the serger - yes, the serger and then machine quilted and hand bound it. I also used some magic stuff called No More Pins so that I didn't have to worry about wrecking blades by serging over any pins. I've written up some instructions for you so you don't have to waste time making mistakes. I think I made most of them as I was working out how to get all the piecing correct.

I used some of the fabric from the Jinny Beyer palette. I thought that as it is an on-going range, you still had a bit of time up your sleeve before you made your quilt (!!!!!!!).The colours are just so right.I remember those few lines from that old magazine we found, about the frontier woman's needs and her dreams.I still think they are the most evocative I've ever read:"I stitched as quickly as I could so my family would not freeze, and as beautifully as I could so my heart would not break".

I can only imagine how our pioneering women would have been today with this terrific fabric, thread and a serger - absolutely squillions of quilts,for beauty and warmth.

Bye For Now
The Sentimental Serger

bushfire quilt

Australia is the driest continent on earth. Periods of prolonged drought wreak havoc to the land, flora and fauna, farmers and in small country towns. Mother Nature's penalty extends as prices and tempers rise and there is still no relief in sight. Everyone unites when the `Total Fire Ban` warning is in force, memories revived of the terror and devastation a bushfire leaves in its wake. The colours of a bushfire are memorable. The Bushfire Quilt is an endeavour in part to capture their essence.

Requirements

Fabric: from the Jinny Beyer palette by RJR:

1.7m (1¾ yd) .... Cinnabar Marble..Red
0.7m (¾ yd) .... Pine Net ....Green
1.2m (1¼ yd)............................... Marble Montage ....Gold
2.2m (2½ yd) .... Colors of Christmas ....Black
0.4m (½ yd)................................. Olive Lampas Rose ....Ochre
5m (5 yd) .... Backing Fabric...

Thread:

- Serger: 4 reels Metrosene to blend with fabric – grey or cream for dark or light fabrics respectively
- Sewing machine: 2 reels Madeira rayon variegated # 2145 for quilt top
- Metrosene to match quilt back
- Madeira Monofilament – Smoke

Universal # 80 needles

Batting:

Nu Wool cut to measure

Rotary cutter, mat and ruler

60 ml/2oz – Craft Smart® No More Pins

Sewing machine, general sewing supplies

¼ inch sewing gauge

Instruction manual for your serger

Description:

Square in a square, set on point

- Serger pieced, machine quilted

Finished size of quilt:

152 cm x 213 cm
(60 in x 84 in)

the bushfire quilt (cont)

Before we start –

The overall size of this quilt depends upon a little practice to perfect technique and to ensure accurate measurements. If you follow these guidelines, serger piecing will mean faster, and even more quilts for you to make (I wouldn't tell the family too soon).

- set the serger for a 4 thread overlock stitch – they will all be baseline settings
- thread with 4 Metrosene threads, grey or cream to blend with your fabric
- cut two 30cm (12in) x 15 cm (6in) fabric strips from your quilt fabric scraps
- place fabric right sides together
- serge the long sides from edge to edge, always cutting off some fabric, even if only a 'whisker'
- using the sewing gauge, measure the overlock stitch. If it measures 6.3mm (¼ in), jump for joy. If not, adjust the cutting width according to the manufacturer's guidelines in your instruction book until the measurement is accurate.

I cannot emphasize too strongly how important this step is – it's not so much of a problem if you're not 100 percent accurate on a sewing machine, reverse sewing (unpicking) is possible. Reverse serging does not really work; believe me, I did enough of it before I worked out it was easier to be precise in the first place.

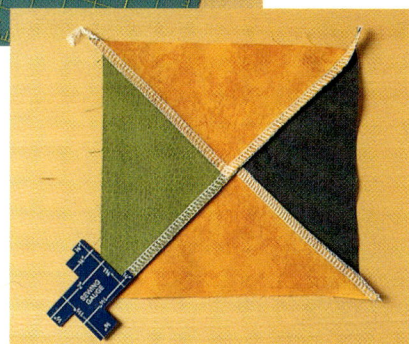

Cutting

From the red fabric:
Large squares & rectangles:
- cut 8 strips 16.5cm (6½ in) wide
- cross-cut strips into 38 x 16.5cm (6½ in) squares
- cross-cut remaining strips at 8.8mm (3½ in) intervals for the rectangles

Small squares:
- cut 4 x 9.8cm (3⅞ in) squares

Borders:
- cut 8 strips 6.3cm (2½ in) wide

From the green fabric:
Large triangles:
- cut 3 strips 18.4cm (7¼ in) wide
- cross-cut into 10 x 18.4cm (7¼ in) squares
- cross-cut on both diagonals to yield 40 quarter-square triangles (2 will not be used)

Small triangles:
- cut 1 strip 9.8cm (3⅞ in) wide
- cross-cut into 6 x 9.8cm (3⅞ in) squares
- cross-cut on the diagonal to yield 12 half-square triangles

From the gold fabric:

Large triangles:
- cut 5 strips 18.4 cm (7¼ in) wide
- cross-cut into 22 x 18.4 cm (7¼ in) squares
- cross-cut on both diagonals to yield 88 quarter-square triangles

Small triangles:
- cut 1 strip 9.8 cm (3⅞ in) wide
- cross-cut into 8 x 9.8 cm (3⅞ in) squares
- cross-cut on the diagonal to yield 16 half-square triangles

From the black fabric:

Large triangles:
- cut 3 strips 18.4 cm (7¼ in) wide
- cross-cut into 10 x 18.4 cm (7¼ in) squares
- cross-cut on both diagonals to yield 40 quarter-square triangles (2 will not be used)

Small triangles:
- cut 1 strip 9.8 cm (3⅞ in) wide
- cross-cut into 6 x 9.8 cm (3⅞ in) squares
- cross-cut on the diagonal to yield 12 half-square triangles

Borders:
- cut 9 strips 8.9 cm (3½ in) wide

Binding:
- cut 9 strips 6.3 cm (2½ in) wide

From the ochre fabric:

Borders:
- cut 8 strips 3.8 cm (1½ in) wide

Piecing

The Bushfire Quilt is pieced in components – because of the nature of the piecing, this experimental "sergery" was more accurate when done this way.

Trust me, I know, I've hidden the first 500 crude attempts; the family are convinced now that their mattresses are in need of replacement.

Put all the small triangles aside for the moment. Take all the gold, green and black large triangles placing them in their colour groups near the serger. There should be twice as many gold triangles as black and green.

- take one gold and one black triangle.
- place right sides together along bias (short) edges, gold fabric uppermost
- serge the fabrics together along the bias edge, from the squared end
- serger piece continuously, joining fabric pairs. This method gives new meaning to chain piecing!! Continue serging until all the gold and black fabric triangles are completed. Open out and press the seam towards the black fabric
- repeat the same step serging the remaining gold and green triangles, continuing to keep the gold triangle uppermost
- open out; press toward the green fabric
- to make the pieced squares, place the 2 sets of triangle pairs in colour groups
- using No More Pins, place a drop on the point of a pin
- place a scant drop at the intersection of both seams, lining up the pairs
- when dry, serge both triangles together, press open – you now have a square

You will now have 38 pieced and 39 plain red squares. Place the 2 groups of squares close to the serger, piecing as follows

- take one plain and one pieced square, right sides together
- keep the pieced square uppermost
- serge a 6mm (¼ in) seam along the edge of the gold fabric with the green triangle to the top
- repeating the last technique, chain serge 33 rectangles: these are the horizontal rectangles, which will be

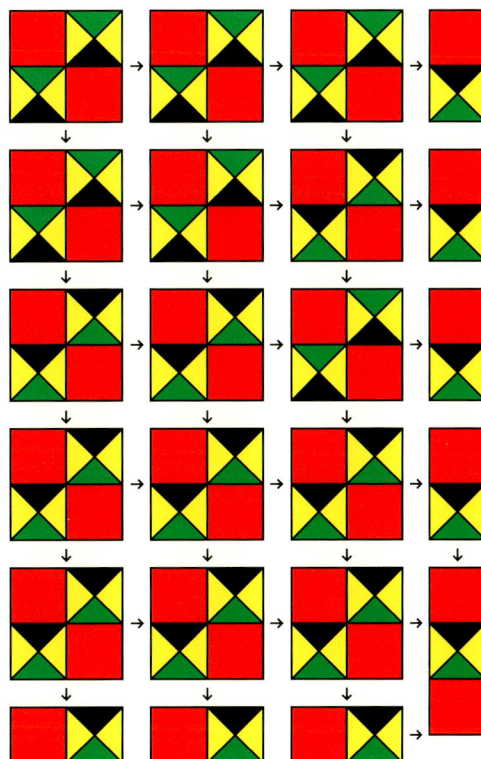

placed across the quilt in rows
- 6 plain and 5 pieced blocks remain
- piece these in pairs, the pieced square uppermost, serging the green fabric edge: this creates vertical rectangles
- serge the remaining plain square to the black fabric edge of a vertical rectangle
- for all rectangles, the seam is pressed towards the red fabric
- using No More Pins match the rectangles, at the intersection – serge into 15 square blocks
- you will have 3 horizontal and 5 vertical rectangles remaining
- serge these together as shown in the following diagram below

Nearly there!!!

If you want to save yourself any more challenges, you can omit the next step. It does, however, complete the block on point.

The outer edge of the block is worked as a pieced border, consisting of flying geese, rectangles and squares. There are 4 different 'geese': the construction is the same for each (I cannot resist – these are the goose steps).

- lay out the triangles out before you sew
- take a large triangle, placing its broadest base towards you as you look at it
- place the small triangles down with the bias edges of all the triangles together – the block is created just not sewn

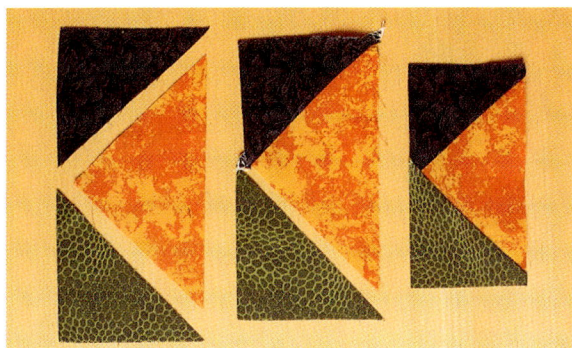

the bushfire quilt (cont)

- place the smaller triangle on top of the larger, right sides together, matching the outer corners – the upper point will extend beyond the edge
- serge the left hand edge of all the blocks, the smaller triangle on top of the larger, right sides together – press toward the small triangle
- place the remaining small triangle on top of the larger, right sides together
- serge the right hand edge of all the blocks, the smaller triangle on top of the larger, press toward the small triangle
- refer to the diagram

You will now have 4 sets of geese – 2 sets of 4 for the top and bottom and 2 sets of 6 for either side. Each set is worked the same way

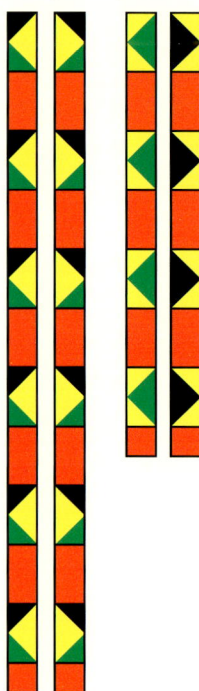

- take one pieced unit and one red rectangle, place right sides together with the pieced unit uppermost
- serge the short sides together. Repeat this step for each set. There will be 2 x 3 and 2 x 4 pairs and 1 pieced unit remaining – put these aside for the moment
- serge the pairs to one another alternating pieced and plain rectangles until there are 4 strips of each set
- press all seams toward the red fabric

- take the remaining pieced rectangles and the 4 small red squares
- place right sides together, the square uppermost
- serge along the short edge of the fabrics
- press toward the red fabric
- serge to the remaining strips and press again. The pieced border is complete, ready to attach
- attach to the top and bottom first
- using 'No More Pins' apply to the intersections. Allow to dry and check that the placement is accurate. Serge with the border strip uppermost, press toward the border
- attach the sides, again using 'No More Pins', apply to the intersections. Allow to dry and check that the placement is accurate. Serge with the border strip uppermost, press toward the border

*All **the really** hard work is now done, time for a Vegemite sandwich*

Attaching the borders

The Ochre Border

- attach the upper and lower borders first
- measure across the width of the quilt at the centre and the top and bottom edge
- cut the border strip to the average of these measurements
- sew the 3.8cm (1½ in) strips together to make up the width and serge to the top and bottom of the quilt. To prevent any shift of fabric, dot the fabric layers with 'No More Pins' if required
- measure through the new length of the quilt at the centre and either side

- sew the 3.8cm (1½ in) strips together to make up the length
- cut the border strip to the average of these measurements then serge to both sides. To prevent any shift of fabric, dot the fabric layers with 'No More Pins' if required

The Red Border

- sew the 6.3cm (2½ in) strips together to make up the width and serge to the top and bottom of the quilt
- repeat the instructions for the ochre border

The Black Border

- sew the 8.9cm (3½ in) strips together to make up the width and serge to the top and bottom of the quilt
- repeat the instructions for the ochre border

Quilting

- take the backing fabric and cut into two lengths of 2.2m (2½ yd)
- serge the entire length, trimming the selvedge
- press the seam to one side
- layer the backing fabric, batting and quilt top
- pin or baste together.

At this stage, give your serger a well-earned clean, oil and rest while you finish the remainder of The Bushfire Quilt on the sewing machine

- insert a new # 80 needle in the machine
- thread the machine with Madeira monofilament(when you're quilting a Bushfire, what else would you use but smoke?)
- wind the bobbin with Metrosene to match the backing fabric

- quilt in the ditch around each of the squares and along each border to hold the sandwich together securely
- thread the machine with Madeira Rayon #2145, a bold variegated thread. The Metrosene in the bobbin does not require changing
- lower the feed dogs and use a combination of stippling and free-motion straight lines to emulate the flames and turmoil created in an intense fire. I quilted heavily – I love doing any form of free motion embroidery where I can create as I go along and don't know when to stop, hence the heavy quilting.

Binding

- thread the machine with Metrosene thread in the needle and bobbin
- sew the nine 6.3cm (2½ in) strips together using 45 degree joins
- press along the length, wrong sides together
- with binding uppermost on the front of the quilt, attach with a 6mm (¼ in) seam, mitreing each corner as you go
- trim any excess batting and backing
- fold the binding to the back of the quilt, slipstitch in place
- label and date your quilt

IT'S FINISHED –
the family can eat again!

At this stage you may like to do a rain dance so you can put out the current bushfire and create another.

Hi J.F.,

Ah, but country life's just great. I went to my very first farm auction the other week, a deceased estate of the last woman from a local family who have been around this area for generations. She was fondly called The Old Maid. You should have seen the stuff! Hay balers, old furniture, books, and separators.

I bought an old box of 'miscellaneous' things, can't resist a bargain. I nearly fell off my chair when I opened it and found some of the treasure inside. Right up our alley! Magnificent old laces, embroideries , batiste, cotton net. The more I looked at it the more I wondered what it was originally intended for. I suspect it was planned for a wedding dress. Whatever could have happened? War? Illness? Something sad ,I think. Maybe that's why everyone has such warmth in their voice when they speak of her, obviously fond memories.

Anyway, I have made a quilt from this magic cornucopia, adding lots of modern trims: lace, Swiss embroideries, insertions, entredeux, beading and batiste .I added some of my little collection of handmade laces. I decided that I had not worked out a way to take it with me to my ultimate resting place when the time came, so I had better use it before the family gave it away probably wondering "What on Earth would Mum have wanted that much for?" I suppose I just don't want it to end up in a box for someone else to wonder about.

I can't copy the unique measurements of the splendid antique trims. I've tried to work around it, but keep on ending up in the conundrum corner. The laces add both luxury and cost - perhaps fewer laces and more fabric technique for the new creation? I suppose the instructions for the quilt as I serged it and the techniques used may be adapted; I can just hear you saying "any which way".

Oh, didn't I tell you? I put myself and (now you no doubt) into heart attack territory and the Sewer's Naughty Corner - you know, you're sent there for not doing things how the traditonalists say they should be done. I joined laces on the serger; serger pieced and machine quilted it.

Sit down before you read the next bit. I put the quilt in the dryer on hot after washing to 'antique' it. If you read it fast you really don't notice what I've done. It worked really well except for my idiocy. I should have quilted the mitred borders much closer; they just don't look quite right in the photo I'm sending. I'll do some more when I don't have to share my time with anyone else.

I've called it the 'Wedding Dress Quilt'. I hope The Old Maid would have liked it; she was often in my thoughts while I was making it. I'll send the instructions as best I can; I will try and do it as components. You might only want to try the centre block as a cushion panel.

Bye for now

PS: I dyed some of my hand-made Venetian lace for a more old fashioned rose look. I think the family is questioning whether I've lost the plot or not. I keep telling them life's too short not to have a go at absolutely, positively everything. What's that wonderful expression? You're a long time dead.

Bye again

The Bridesmaid

the wedding dress quilt

Select a variety of laces, fabrics or simple embellishment from other items in Serging Australia to create your own Wedding Dress Quilt. If you are fortunate enough to own an embroidery machine, a delicate design in the centre of the borders may be your choice. Hand embroidery also offers limitless possibilities. Use and enjoy your laces and fabric where you can see them.

Requirements – Fabric-Swiss batiste

For medallion underlay	2.2m (2½ yd) ..1.06m (42 in) wide White or Ecru
For medallion	0.9m (1 yd) ....1.06m (42 in) wide White batiste
	0.9m (1 yd) ......1.06m (42 in) wide Ecru batiste
For mitred corners	1.8m (2yd)......1.06m (42 in) wide White batiste
	90cm (1yd) ......1.06m (42 in) wide Ecru batiste
Backing	3m (2¾ yd) ....1.06m (42 in) wide White or Ecru batiste
Binding	60cm (⅔ yd) ....1.06m (42 in) wide Ecru batiste

I have given fabric requirements for each of the quilt components: your personal requirements will vary depending upon which of the components you use. The entire quilt will use nearly 50% less overall than these individual components.

Variety of 100% cotton trimmings and Swiss embroideries, lace insertion, beading, beading insertion, White and Ecru

Thread:
- Serger: 6 reels Madeira Cotona 50, #504
- Sewing Machine: 1 reel Madeira Cotona 50, #504

Needles:

Universal # 70

Spray starch or fabric finish
Avalon™ water soluble stabilizer
Craft Smart® No More Pins
Water soluble marker

Batting:

Fairfield 'Soft Touch' 100% cotton batting

Rotary cutter, mat and ruler
Instruction manual for your serger
Continuous gum leaf design (see page 31)

Description

100 % cotton Heirloom Medallion quilt
- Serger pieced, machine quilted

Finished size of quilt

1.5m (60 in) x 1.5m (60 in) approximately

the wedding dress quilt (cont)

Before you start –

Take the time and a few pieces of fabric and lace to practice. Time spent now saves a lot of frustration later on. When you get the hang of these techniques, this is fantastically fast serging.

There are only 2 techniques used in The Wedding Dress quilt: Rolled hem flatlock and rolled hem. The medallion and subsequent borders are strip pieced and then cross cut to form the components of the quilt.

Rolled hem flatlock

You will probably not find this stitch in your manual: it is the finest of overlock stitches yet surprisingly strong. It is simply a result of my dissatisfaction with the raised seam achieved using a standard rolled hem to join these light materials. I played at the serger until I was satisfied with the method for the quilt. The ladder that is formed with this flatlock is so fine I serged it to finish uppermost. If you can see to thread the ladder please do. My eyes have reached a degree of maturity that they tend to think this is best left to the young and passionate.

please note not all sergers are able to adapt to this stitch setting, having a pre-set needle/length/tension ratio that cannot be over-ridden. The standard rolled hem or narrow 3 thread stitch are adequate – practice to determine which you prefer.

Refer to your serger manual for specific flatlock settings; try them with the set up for rolled hem and record them when satisfied

L.N.	R.N.	U.L.	L.L.
-----	Very loose	Baseline	Tighten
S.L.	D.F.	C.W.	Sp.
1-1½	Neutral	Rolled hem setting	Change foot & plate if necessary.

Lace to lace:
- select a variety of patterns and widths of 100% cotton insertion lace-the lace does not have to be continuous lengths, 15cm (6 in) strips can be serged to a fabric strip
- cut fabric strips selvedge to selvedge. Trim the selvedge edges from the fabric
- lightly spray starch the laces and fabric to be joined
- place right sides together
- using Avalon™ as a leader, serge strips of lace & fabric together. The needle should be just to the left of the header threads – check your reference markings
- gently pull the lace and fabric apart, leaving the stabilizer in place-this will be removed when the strips are cross cut

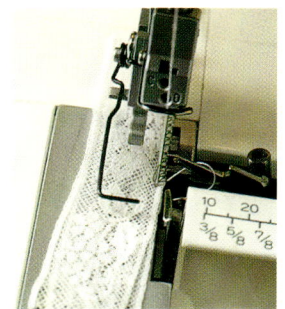

Foot retaining spring left in place to give a reference point for your serging.

the wedding dress quilt (cont)

Entredeux to fabric

- select a range of entredeux – the entredeux does not have to be continuous lengths, 15cm (6 in) strips can be serged to a fabric strip
- cut fabric strips selvedge to selvedge. Trim the selvedge edges from the fabric
- lightly spray starch the fabric to be joined to the entredeux
- place right sides together, entredeux uppermost, fabric edges together
- using Avalon™ as a leader, serge strips of fabric and entredeux together. The needle should be just to the right of the entredeux, trimming off the batiste edge – check your reference markings for needle placement
- gently pull the entredeux and fabric apart, leaving the stabilizer in place – this will be removed when the strips are cross cut

Entredeux to lace

- select a range of entredeux and lace
- lightly spray starch the lace to be joined to the entredeux
- place right sides together, lace uppermost

The needle should be just to the right of the entredeux and just to the left of the lace heading, trimming off the batiste edge – check your reference markings for needle placement. Refer to the photo (above left), a picture is worth its weight in gold for this technique

- using Avalon™ as a leader, serge strips of fabric and entredeux together
- gently pull the entredeux and lace apart, leaving the stabilizer in place – this will be removed when the strips are cross cut

Rolled hem

L.N.	R.N.	U.L.	L. L.
-----	Baseline or little looser	Baseline or little looser	Tighten
S.L.	D.F.	C.W.	Sp.
1-2	Neutral	Rolled hem setting	Change foot & plate if necessary.

The rolled hem is the perfect stitch to create either raised or concealed tucks on very fine fabrics. It is easy to become a sergerholic with the speed you can go with this technique. As with any tucks, an odd number is visually more pleasing. There are 2 methods used in The Wedding Dress Quilt

Method # 1 – used for joining separate pieces and different colours of fabric
- cut fabric strips selvedge to selvedge. Trim the selvedge edges from the fabric
- with wrong sides of fabric together, serge a rolled hem from edge to edge. It is unlikely that you will need the Avalon™ leader but use it if you prefer

Method # 2 – used to create tucks in the centre of a fabric strip
- fold fabric in half selvedge to selvedge
- press firmly to crease along the fold line

- serge the length of the creased fabric, along the fold
- turn the fabric so that you will start at the end where you have just finished
- using the serger foot as your guide, serge the second tuck parallel to the first. Butt the foot so that it is touching the tuck, serge, folding the fabric under as you go
- Continue creating sets of odd numbered tucks in this manner alternating the end at which you start to prevent puckering. The tucks will not all be rolling in the same direction but they are very fine and with odd numbers the effect is unnoticeable

Let's start to make this a bit prettier than it is just now

The components

The construction of the components is now at hand. The size and technique used in each unit is given

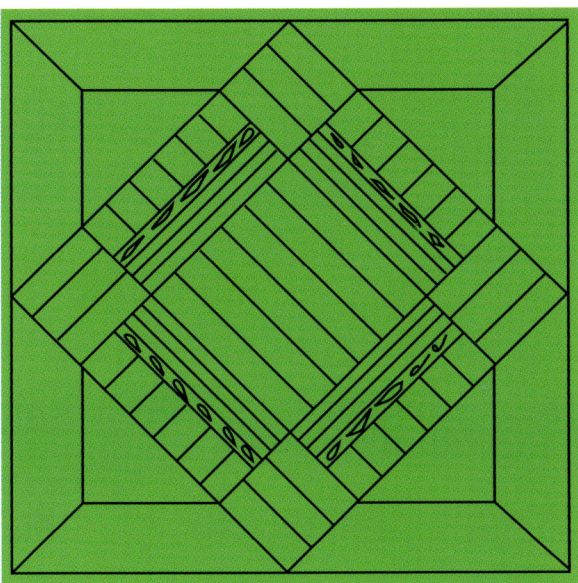

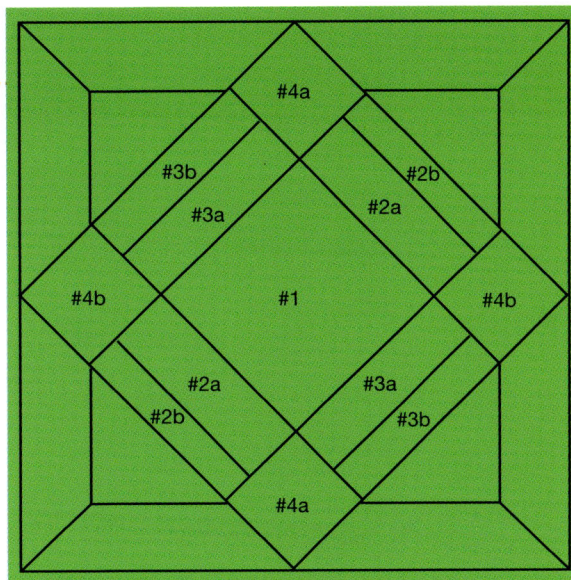

The Medallion-# 1

- made of lace to lace strips, rolled hem flatlocked to a measurement of 26cm (10¼ in) x 26cm (10¼ in). Borders were added to the top and bottom, then either side to frame the heart of the quilt and make it 44.5cm (17½ in) x 44.5cm (17½ in) in square (43cm/17 in finished); refer to the technique of 'attaching borders' in the Bushfire Quilt project. You may prefer to add a plain fabric border to embellish.

Borders-#2a #2b

- #2a – alternate long strips of white and ecru with rolled hem pintucks, plain fabric either side to a measurement of 17.8cm (7 in) x 44.5cm (17½ in) (16.5cm/6½ in x 43cm/17 in finished) tucks uppermost
- #2b – alternate short strips of rolled hem pintucks, lace, entredeux, fabric to a measurement of 14cm (5½ in) x 44.5cm (17½ in) (12.7cm/5 in x 43cm/17 in finished) tucks uppermost
- serge together along the long edge, to create a unit measuring 30.5cm (12 in) x 44.5cm (17½ in) (29.2cm/11½ in x 43cm/17 in finished)

Wedding Dress Quilt

Finished appearance

the wedding dress quilt (cont)

Borders – #3a #3b

- #3a – alternate long strips of white and ecru with rolled hem pintucks, plain fabric either side to a measurement of 17.8cm (7 in) x 44.5cm (17½ in) (16.5cm/6½ in x 43cm/17in finished) tucks to the underside
- #3b – alternate short strips of rolled hem pintucks, lace, entredeux, fabric to a measurement of 14cm (5½ in) x 44.5cm (17½ in) (12.7cm/5 in x 43cm/17in finished) tucks to the underside
- serge together along the long edge, to create a unit measuring 30.5cm (12 in) x 44.5cm (17½ in) (29.2cm/11½ in x 43cm/17in finished)

Borders – #4a #4b

- strips of laces with borders added, to a measurement of 30.5cm (12 in) x 30.5cm (12 in) (29.2cm/11½ in x 29.2cm/11½ in in finished)
- # 4a – the laces run parallel to the centre medallion
- # 4b – the laces run perpendicular to the centre medallion

Follow the piecing diagram to join the components. Add a 3.8cm (1½ in) (2.5cm/1 in finished) border around the pieced square to end up with a quilt centre 1.06m (42 in) x 1.06m (42 in)

Underlay

The medallion requires an underlay to support the quilting. Try both the white and ecru before cutting out to see which you prefer

- take the underlay fabric and cut into two lengths of 1.1m (1¼ yd)

- serge the entire length with a 4 thread stitch, trimming the selvedge
- press the seam to one side
- decide where you would prefer your seam to lay then trim the overlay to 1.9m (43 in) sq
- using the sewing machine, baste the medallion and the underlay together.

They will now be treated as the medallion piece

> *One bit out of the way!*
> *Sit down, have a cuppa, and admire your handiwork.*
> *You've earned it.*

The mitred corners

At last, the beginning of the end.
Fabric requirements for mitred corners:
White – 1.8m (2yd) (110cm/42 in wide)
Ecru – 90cm (1yd) (110cm/42 in wide)

Cutting

The outer mitred corners are made from 3 fabric strips, embellished with 5 rows each of rolled hem tucks. They measure: white 21.6cm (8½ in) ecru 16.5cm (6½ in) and ecru with lace 6.3cm (2½ in) cut (20.3, 15.2, 5.1 cm/8,6,2 in finished)

please note these strips are very wide and would be more aesthetically pleasing made smaller. I do not reverse serge and will quilt them more heavily on my quilt to fill in the wide-open paddocks (fields) I created.

- make 2 templates from paper as a guide. They will be identical but mirror imaged measuring 80cm (31½ in) cut (76.2cm/30 in finished) along the outer edge

the wedding dress quilt (cont)

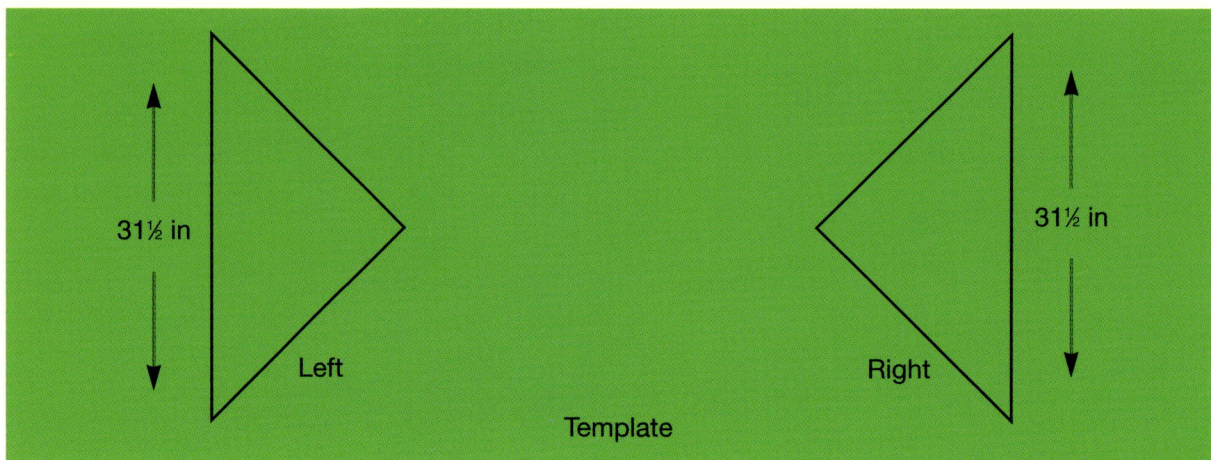

31½ in   Left   Right   31½ in

Template

- mark one as Left, the other as Right
- lay out the 2 templates
- lay your fabric strips in an offset manner and place a mark at the point where the 2 fabric strips are to join, as per the diagram

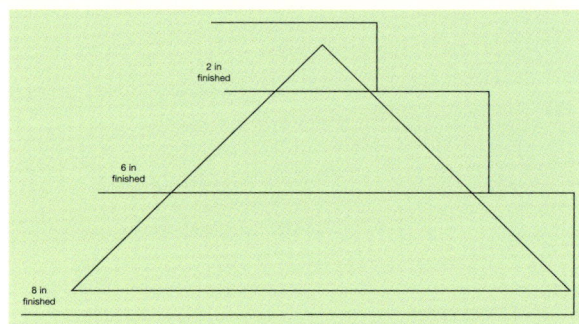

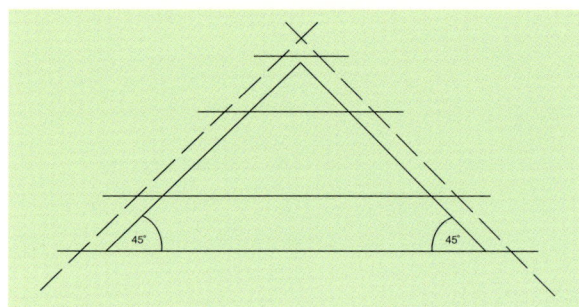

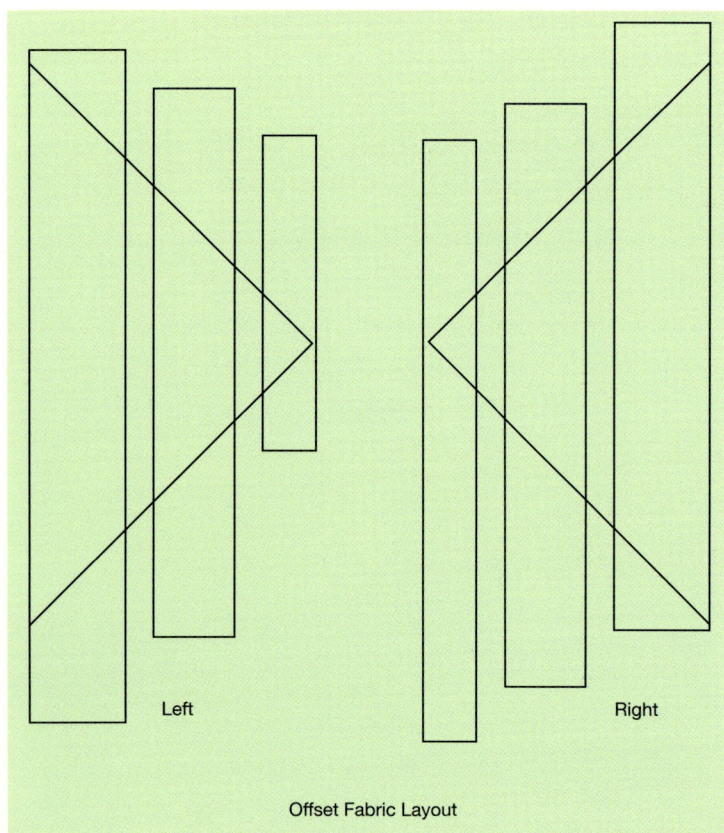

Offset Fabric Layout

Left   Right

- serge these strips together
- spray lightly with spray starch, press
- lay on paper template, checking accuracy
- cut at 45⁰ angle to outer long edge *-note-* you may have to cut half way and then carefully reposition the ruler to cut the remainder
- turn the ruler over and repeat for the other side
- continue to cut in the same manner until you have 1 of each per corner

Piecing

- take 1 right and 1 left corner piece
- place right sides together
- dot with No More Pins™, carefully matching rows of tucks and fabric colours
- serge the edges together using a 4 thread stitch, press

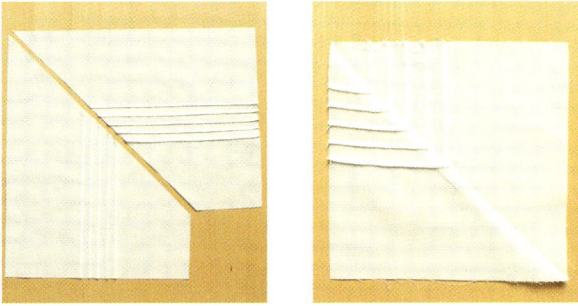

- you now have 4 corners and are nearly finished the quilt top
- take one corner piece and lay on the medallion, long side to the medallion edge
- serge together, press
- repeat for the opposite side and then the remaining 2 sides

The Wedding Dress Quilt is now preparing for marriage. . .

Quilting

- take the backing fabric and cut into two lengths of 1.5m(1⅝ yd)
- serge the entire length, trimming the selvedge
- press the seam to one side
- layer the backing fabric, batting, and quilt top
- pin or baste together.

Give your serger a clean, oil and rest while you finish the remainder of The Wedding Dress

Quilt on the sewing machine

- insert a new # 70 needle in the machine
- thread the machine with Cotona 50, # 504
- wind the bobbin with the Cotona also
- quilt in the ditch around each of the squares and along the lace seams to hold the sandwich together securely
- transfer the continuous gum leaf design to the plain fabric in border component # 2a. You may like to also quilt the mitred borders
- lower the feed dogs and use a free-motion straight line to stitch the gum leaf design

Binding

- sew the eight 6.3cm (2½ in) strips together using 45 degree joins
- press along the length, wrong sides together
- place binding uppermost on the front of the quilt
- attach the binding with a 6mm (¼ in) seam, mitreing each corner as you go
- trim any excess batting and backing
- fold the binding to the back of the quilt, slipstitch in place
- label and date your quilt

Your Wedding Dress Quilt is now ready for the trip down the aisle. Don't be surprised if you never get away for your honeymoon as everyone admires your handiwork. Please enjoy this special quilt.

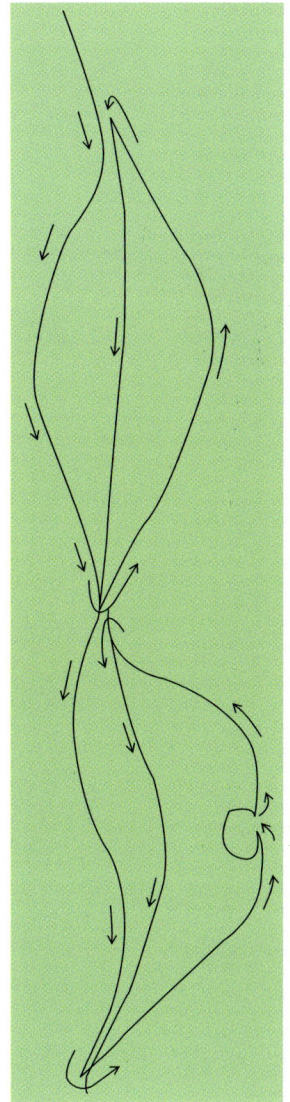

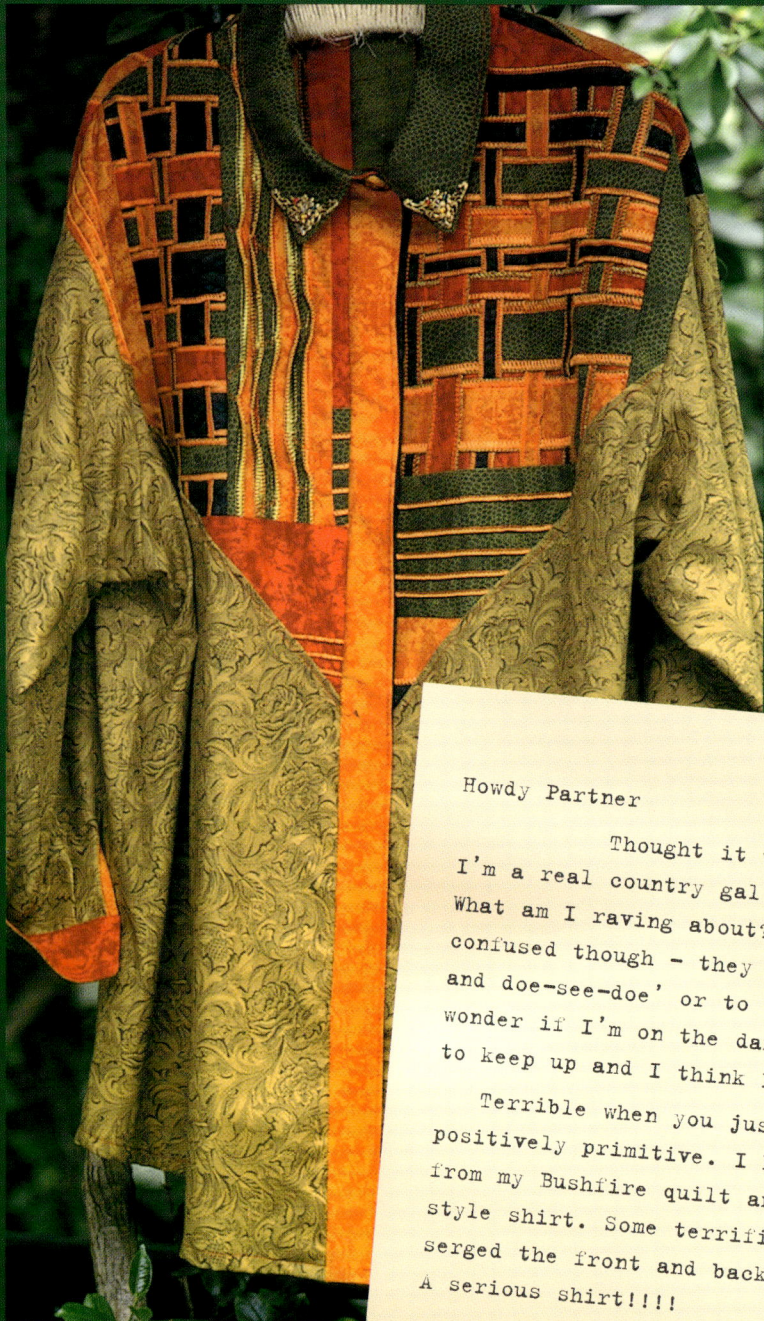

Howdy Partner

    Thought it was time to catch up with y'all again. Well I'm a real country gal now, and its either 'be there or be square'. What am I raving about? Dancing of course. My feet are really confused though – they don't know whether to 'take your partner and doe-see-doe' or to 'heel, toe, heel, toe and buttermilk'. I wonder if I'm on the dance floor or in the dairy! Anyway I'm trying to keep up and I think I'm part way there.

    Terrible when you just don't have a thing to wear though. I felt positively primitive. I had some practice and odd pieces left over from my Bushfire quilt and thought I'd better make up a 'country' style shirt. Some terrific thread, a little bit of play, and I serged the front and back tops, designing as I went. Yeohhhhhhhhh! A serious shirt!!!!

    My shirt will take me from our country music capital, Tamworth, to that other semi-quaver on the country music pilgrimage, Nashville. You guys have got some catching up to do though – we are in the record books for the largest number of boot-scooters dancing, or is it scooting (?) to the same tune at once. I think we take it turn about – when the big Nashville festival is on you get the record back aaaandoe-see-doe on.

    Until I tried it, I didn't know you could dance with two left feet! Will send you the instructions. No, not the dancing, the shirt !!!!

    Bye from Boot Scootersville

tamworth to nashville
- a country shirt

The country dance has always been a firm community favourite, whether a Woolshed dance after shearing was finished, a Picnic Race Day finale or a B&S (bachelor and spinster) 'bash' for the young hopefuls. 'All or nothing' energy and flair were exhibited on the dance floor. The growth and popularity of Country Music has kept up pace equally with the passion of boot scootin' and square dancing. A country shirt will be equally at home from Tamworth to Nashville and on any dance floor.

Requirements

McCalls Pattern # 6961, view A

Fabric: from the Jinny Beyer palette by RJR:

Olive Lampas Rose ....Ochre..as per pattern for main body and sleeves

Cinnabar Marble .... Red – 25cm (¼yd) .... for collars and sleeves

Pine Net ....Green – 25cm (¼yd) .... for collars and sleeves

Marble Montage ....Gold – 45cm (½yd) ....for cut on facings

Colors of Christmas ....Black – 45 cm (½yd) ....for cut on facings

Interfacing as per pattern

Thread: Serger: Metrosene –
4 reels to blend for fabric for construction

- Décor # 1478, # 1540
- Madeira Rayon # 1037

Needles: Universal # 80

Craft Smart® Fray Stop

Craft Smart® No More Pins

Rotary cutter, mat and ruler

Sewing machine, general sewing supplies

Tracing paper

Instruction manual for your serger

Description:

Country style shirt with embellished basket weave and crazy patchwork front and back yokes

tamworth to nashville
- a country shirt (cont)

Cutting

Cut out the main body of the shirt and the sleeves from the ochre fabric

Cut out 1 collar and 1 neckband from both the red and green fabric

Cut out 2 red and 2 green cuffs

Cut out 2 gold continuous laps

Cut out 1 gold and 1 black front facing – the fabric will have to be placed across the fabric, selvedge to selvedge

Put all the shirt pieces aside while you make the embellished yokes. These will be made according to the pattern, no shirt construction is given.

The remaining fabric will now be embellished to create your yoke.

Method

Before you start –

that's right, have a practice first to perfect the technique. The time saved by eliminating the gremlins is mind boggling. My mind boggles at the thought of not doing it first – not a pretty sight, I can assure you.

Cut a variety of strips from the 4 yoke fabrics, varying the width. Short pieces and odd shapes all work well. Vary the thread colour and technique to make your personalized country shirt

3 thread wide with Decor thread

L.N.	R.N.	U.L.	L.L.
Baseline	-----	Looser	Baseline

S.L.	D.F.	C.W.	Sp.
2½-3½	Neutral	Baseline	

3 thread narrow with Decor thread

L.N.	R.N.	U.L.	L.L.
-----	Baseline	Looser	Baseline

S.L.	D.F.	C.W.	Sp.
2-3	Neutral	Baseline	Change plate & foot if necessary

use to edge fabric strips

3 thread flatlock with Decor thread

L.N.	R.N.	U.L.	L.L.
Very Loose	-----	Looser	Baseline

S.L.	D.F.	C.W.	Sp.*
2-3	Neutral	Baseline	Lower cutting blade if preferred

*See note in 'technical stuff'

• use to join strips of fabric embellishment or different coloured fabrics

3 thread rolled hem with Decor thread

L.N.	R.N.	U.L.	L.L.
-----	Baseline	Looser	Tighten

S.L.	D.F.	C.W.	Sp.
2-3	Neutral	Rolled hem	Change foot & plate if necessary

• serge sets rolled hem tucks across a wide band of fabric. Odd numbers work best

3 thread wide with Decor thread – Upper and Lower Looper

L.N.	R.N.	U.L.	L.L.
Baseline	-----	Looser	Looser

S.L.	D.F.	C.W.	Sp.
2½-3½	Neutral	Baseline	

• serge in sets across a wide band of fabric. Odd numbers work best.
  Use the sewing machine to create 'Mexican' tucks. Sew across the tuck,
  with a straight or decorative stitch and using Madeira rayon in the needle.
  Alternate the direction you sew over the tuck to create a wave like pattern

A Country Shirt

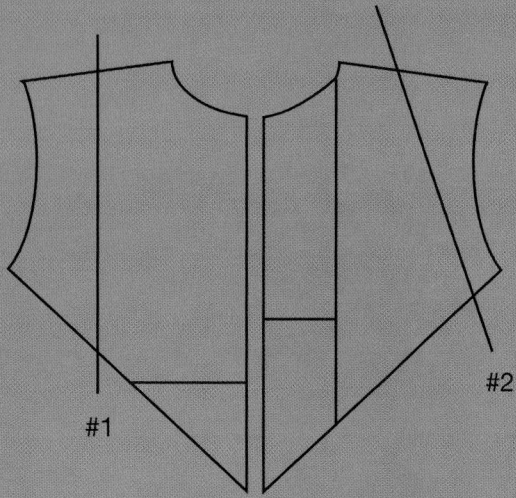

Front

#1

#2

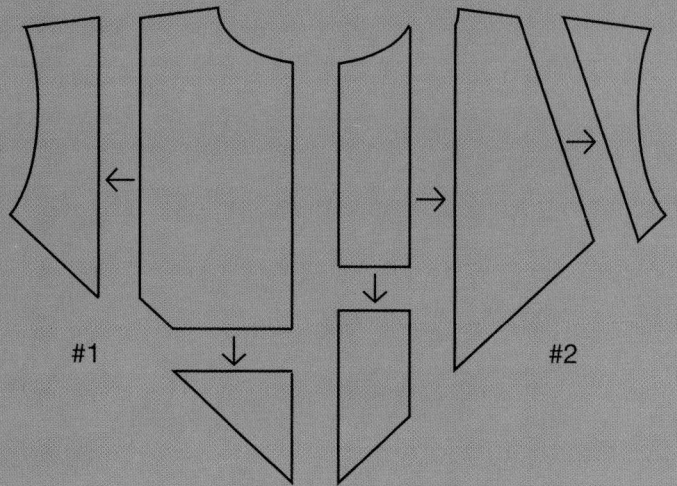

#1

#2

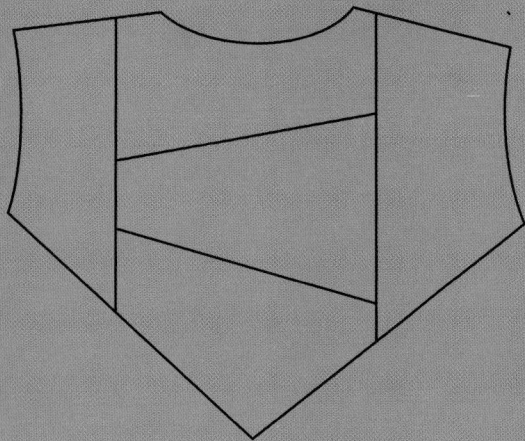

Back

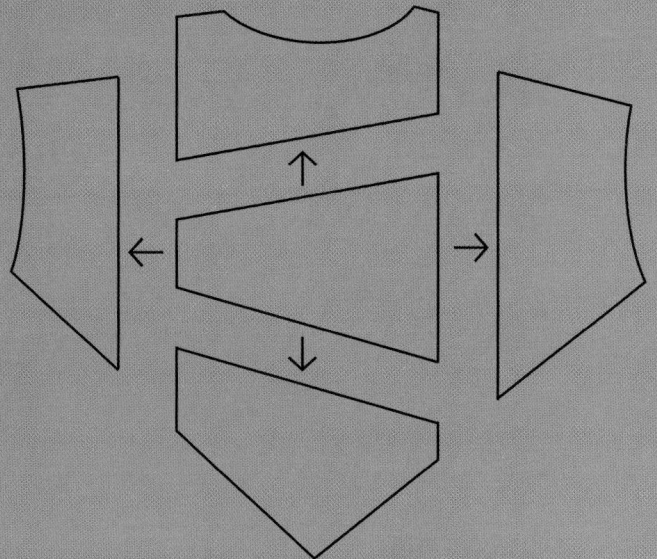

tamworth to nashville
- a country shirt (cont)

Thread the serger for the technique of your choice. In all the techniques, I have used rayon thread in the needle. A subtle emphasis is given to the heavier threads with this technique.

- cut fabric strips selvedge to selvedge; cut selvedge off or use the off cuts from the shirt to create your preferred length and shape
- serge the edges or create sets of stitches from a variety of fabric strips, right side uppermost, chaining off the end of the fabric
- place a dot of Fray Stop on the ends of each of the thread chains closest to the fabric
- trim the excess chain once the sealant is completely dry

Piecing the yoke

- cut 2 pattern fronts and 1 complete pattern back from tracing paper
- cut each into 3 or 4 sections, referring to the diagram (see left page)
- arrange the embellished fabrics on the small pattern pieces until you are satisfied with the layout
- weave a variety of strips of fabric together, varying the width and colour of the strips. Place a dot of 'No More Pins' on the intersecting fabrics to prevent them shifting
- when satisfied with the layout, serge the sections back together with either a decorative flatlock for surface embellishment or a 4 thread stitch for a simpler finish

Finishing

Collar /neckband / cuffs / facings: plan the colour layout to add variety and individuality to your shirt. Construct according to pattern instruction.

Darlin', just sit back, catch your breath and wait for the compliments.

the glory

Hi JF,

Sorry I haven't written for a while, life goes on as busy as ever. It probably wouldn't surprise you that I've been absolutely 'flat out like a lizard drinking', sewing again. School uniforms, clothes, P.J.'s (pyjamas), boxer shorts, all the really necessary boring stuff, but at least it's fast on the serger. When I finally finished, I decided I needed to do something really nice, not just something useful.

Remember the Wedding Dress Quilt? I had some fabric and lace left over and didn't want to make another quilt or a cushion. I made another shirt, same style as the 'Tamworth to Nashville' - saves cutting out another pattern, lazy eh?

I'm tickled pink with how it has turned out - very dressy if I want to go out on the town or great style to wear with jeans. The laces and fabrics are from 'The Old Maid's' glory box; you know how you collect things for when you get married - isn't that what you call a hope chest? Maybe my imagination is carrying me away again.

Perhaps I'll ultimately re-cycle it before it gets too worn and then make that cushion. Dare I say I did the piecing of the panels on the serger using the chain stitch and some Decor thread and worked it on some cotton net, which I also found in the glory box. I think I enjoy working out how to do the difficult pieces (you know the technical bits) as much as the final construction.

Thank you for the Hugs and Kisses. I only gave the family one packet though, the rest is in the sewing room and no-one is game to touch any thing in there. Will send some general instructions for the shirt. I hope you enjoy making this one as much as I did.

Hugs and kisses
The Choc-a-holic serger

box shirt

the glory box shirt

Wishing and praying and thinking and hoping…the beginning of an old 60's song. Sounds like the dreams of a young woman as she collects finery for her future to be put away carefully in her Glory Box. Ah, if only we could do it all again, would we change anything? Who knows?

Requirements

McCall's Pattern # 6961, view A

Fabric: Swiss batiste, 115cm (42 in) wide

    Ecru – as per pattern for the main body of the shirt plus extra 20cm (¼yd)

    White – as required for contrast plus extra 90cm (1 yd)

Swiss Cotton Netting: 20cm (¼yd) of both Ecru and White

Variety of 100% cotton trimmings and Swiss embroideries, lace insertion, beading, beading insertion, White and Ecru

Wide lace edging

Interfacing as per pattern

Thread: 4 reels Cotona # 504

    Madeira Décor # 1455

    Madeira Rayon # 1067

    4 reels Metrosene for construction

Universal # 70 needles

Spray starch or fabric finish

Avalon™ water soluble stabilizer

Water soluble marking pen

Rotary cutter, mat and ruler

Sewing machine, general sewing supplies

Instruction manual for your serger

Description

100% cotton heirloom shirt with serger pieced yokes and serger, machine, and hand embellishment

PLEASE NOTE

The centre back of the shirt is made from surplus pieces from the Wedding Dress Quilt and specific techniques will not be reproduced or you will need a block and tackle to lift this book. Please use whichever of the techniques you prefer to make your shirt unique

Cutting

- cut out the main body of the shirt and the sleeves from the ecru fabric
- cut out 2 front yokes from the white fabric
- cut out 1 back yoke from the white fabric
- cut out 4 white cuffs, after completion of tucks
- cut out 2 ecru continuous laps
- cut out 2 white front facings – the fabric will have to be placed across the fabric, selvedge to selvedge
- cut out 1 neckband from the both the ecru and white fabric

The Collar:

- cut out 1 rectangle each of fabric and net which the collar piece will fit, allowing 2.5cm (1 in) all round
- cut out 1 collar from the embellished rectangle
- cut out 1 collar from the ecru fabric

Put all the shirt pieces aside while you make the embellished yokes. These will be made up according to the pattern; no shirt construction is given.

The remaining fabric will now be embellished to create your yoke.

Setup

- thread the serger for a 3 thread rolled hem with Cotona 50 # 504 thread

3 thread rolled hem

L.N.	R.N.	U.L.	L.L.
-----	Baseline or little looser	Baseline or little looser	Tighten
S.L.	D.F.	C.W.	Sp.
1-2	Neutral	Rolled hem setting	Change foot & plate if necessary

The rolled hem is the perfect stitch to create either raised or concealed tucks on very fine fabrics. As with any tucks, an odd number is visually more pleasing.

Method

Create tucks in the centre of a fabric strip

- cut 20 cm (¼yd) white fabric selvedge to selvedge
- fold fabric in half selvedge to selvedge
- press firmly to crease along the fold line
- serge the length of the creased fabric, along the fold, chain off
- turn the fabric so that you will start at the end where you have just finished
- using the serger foot as your guide, serge the second tuck parallel to the first. Butt the foot so that it is touching the tuck, serge, folding the fabric under as you go
- continue creating sets of odd numbered tucks in this manner alternating the end at which you start to prevent puckering, press

The tucks will not all be rolling in the same direction but they are very fine and with odd numbers the effect is unnoticeable. Cut out 2 cuffs and place with the shirt pieces. Set aside the remainder of the tucked pieces for the time being

The Glory Box Shirt

Setup

- set up your serger for the chain stitch
- thread the needle with the rayon thread, the chain looper with the Decor thread

CHAIN STITCH

NEEDLE	LOOPER
Baseline	Baseline
S.L.	Sp
3-4	Spool net cover if required

Method

- cut 20 cm (8 in) fabric strips selvedge to selvedge
- trim the selvedge edges from the fabric
- cut cotton net the same width as the fabric strips
- retain some netting to remain unadorned
- lightly spray starch the fabric and the net
- using Avalon™ as a leader place under the presser foot
- chain stitch on:
      the net
      the net overlaid on the tucked fabric
      the fabric
      combinations of both
- try either straight lines or curves
- continue until satisfied with the number of strips
- put aside

The Collar:

- take the net and collar rectangle that you have previously cut out
- plan where you would like your chain stitch
- mark straight lines with water-soluble marker
- repeat the above steps
- rinse the fabric in running water to remove all traces of the marker pen
- dry and press
- put back with the other shirt pieces

Rolled hem flatlock

Please note: not all sergers are able to adapt to this stitch setting, having a pre-set needle/length/tension ratio that cannot be over-ridden. The standard rolled hem or narrow 3 thread stitches are adequate – practice to determine which you prefer. Refer to your serger manual for specific flatlock settings; try them with the set up for rolled hem and record them when satisfied

Setup

- thread the serger for rolled hem flatlock with Cotona 50 # 504

Rolled hem flatlock

L.N.	R.N.	U.L.	L.L.
-----	Very Loose	Baseline	Tighten
S.L.	**D.F.**	**C.W.**	**Sp.**
1-1½	Neutral	Rolled hem setting	Change plate & foot if necessary

The yokes of the Glory Box Shirt are made from the strips of fabric you have just made. Entredeux beading is applied either side of the fabric or plain net. The strips are then cross cut and more entredeux is applied. Plain fabric or net can be interspersed to vary the look and reduce the amount of entredeux required.

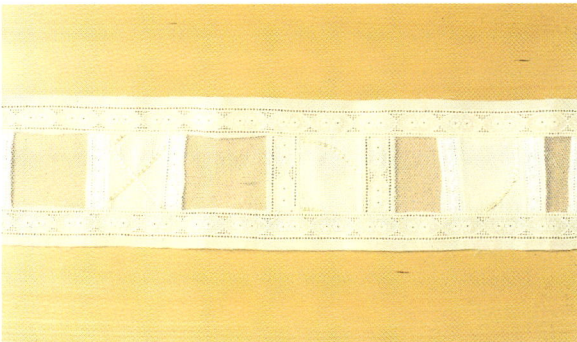

Entredeux to fabric

-note- refer to the photo for this technique in the Wedding Dress Quilt

- select a range of entredeux – the entredeux does not have to be continuous lengths, 15 cm (6 in) strips can be serged to any of your strips
  - place right sides together, entredeux uppermost, fabric edges together
  - using Avalon™ as a leader, serge strips of fabric and entredeux together
  - the needle should be just to the right of the entredeux, trimming off the batiste edge – check your reference markings for needle placement
- gently pull the entredeux and fabric apart, leaving the stabilizer in place – this will be removed when the strips are cross cut

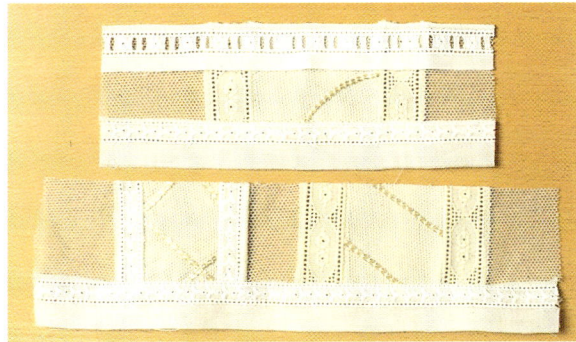

the
glory box shirt (cont)

Piecing of the yokes

- make 2 templates of the front yokes and 1 of the back yoke from paper
- the fronts will be identical but mirror imaged
- mark one as Left, the other as Right
- lay out the 3 templates
- lay your embellished and plain fabric strips in an offset manner and place a mark at the point where the fabric strips are to join (refer to the diagram in The Wedding Dress Quilt)
- serge these strips together
- lay on paper template, checking accuracy
- cut as per pattern
- using the machine, sew to the fabric fronts and backs, as an underlay – they will now be treated as the yoke

The real fun bit is now done: completing your shirt is the ultimate reward for your effort. Your serger is now back to everyday use and should be cleaned, oiled and rethreaded as a 4 thread with Metrosene to match the predominant fabric

Finishing

- join the shirt yokes and the main body of the shirt as per the pattern
- thread the sewing machine with Cotona 50, # 504 in the needle and the bobbin
- apply wide edging lace to all the yokes with a zigzag stitch, length 1cm (⅜ in), width 2.5cm (1 in) making a tuck in the centre back
- using the sewing machine, feather stitch the plain fabric edges on the back yoke
- make the cuffs from a strip of fabric with rolled hem tucks
- construct the remainder of the shirt according the pattern
- add some hand embroidered flowers and delicate greenery and. . .

Que sera sera,
whatever will be will be.

the sumptuous swag

Hi JF,

I know this a about a century overdue, my turn to write, I've been busy with the normal trappings of life – school, sports, ferrying children between their social engagements, keeping the whole lot together. Not a problem!! I've been so busy that my hair has decided to self streak, yes the dreaded grey hair has finally struck: however the grey hair doesn't like the environment either at the moment and is falling out. I think I'll pack up and leave home for a while and go bush.

I've just made my swag, so I'm ready. Just knew you'd ask; a swag is the 'hold all' on the end of a stick, carried over your shoulder. I drew a picture for you. I think mine is rather voluptuous (a bit like me) or perhaps sumptuous is the word; that's it, 'The Sumptuous Swag'. Big enough to hold life's essentials, have serger will travel.

I had this fabulous piece of ultra fine Italian wool and matched it by blending thread colours on the edge. You know me JF, never one to stop at something so simple, I tried a fringed edging, a bit like crochet. On the serger of course. I made some braid and then couched it on by sewing machine. But wait there's more! If enough wasn't enough, I hand-sewed some crystals from a broken necklace I had. And I wonder why the grey hairs don't stick around. I think you'll like it.

I actually wear it as a shawl, not a swag – the stick kept on snagging my clothes. It's fabulous in the winter. I'll send some instructions, I can just see you using it as a sewing holdall – maybe you'd better make two.

Bye from the old grey mare

the sumptuous swag

The swag is probably most regularly associated with that often sung tribute to our colonial past, Waltzing Matilda. The legendary jolly swagman "sang as he sat and waited till his billy boiled". Now, had he been a pioneering woman instead, she would have "sang as she serged and waited till the meal was done."

Requirements

Fabric: Lightweight wool squared to the width of the fabric

Madeira Decor	# 1558	....
....	# 1456	....
Madeira Rayon..................................	# 1173	..................Metrosene thread to match
Universal...	# 80	....

Avalon™ water soluble fabric

Water soluble marker

Craft Smart® Fray Stop

Craft Smart® No More Pins

Spray starch or fabric finish

Chalk marker

Crystals or beads, needle and thread

Rotary cutter, ruler and mat

Sewing machine, general sewing supplies, open-toe foot

Instruction manual for your serger

Description

Oversized woollen shawl with serger matched edging and Cornelli couching

Before you start –

there is no spare fabric allowed in this garment. The price I paid was memorable, so much so that I determined every thread was going to be used. Please perfect your technique on a similar fabric first.

the sumptuous swag (cont)

Setup

- thread your serger for 3 thread wide with Decor in the upper and lower loopers, rayon in the needle

3 thread wide with Decor thread – *Upper and Lower Looper*

L.N.	R.N.	U.L.	L.L.
Baseline	-----	Looser	Looser
S.L.	**D.F.**	**C.W.**	**Sp.**
2½-3½	Neutral	Baseline	

Method

- rotary cut the fabric until square, trimming the selvedges
- lightly spray fabric with spray starch, press
- serge along the first edge of the fabric trimming only a whisker as you go
- serge until the needle is at the end of the fabric
- raise the presser foot; gently ease the threads off the stitch finger
- turn the fabric, ready to serge the second edge
- lower the needle by hand so that it enters the fabric into the outer edge of the previous row of stitching
- lower the presser foot, serge
- repeat these steps until all edges are serged, chain off

- place a dot of Fray Stop on the chain, next to the fabric
- trim the chain when the sealant is dry

Setup

- rethread the serger for a rolled hem with Decor thread

3 thread rolled hem with Decor thread

Method

L.N.	R.N.	U.L.	L.L.
-----	Baseline	Looser	Tighten
S.L.	**D.F.**	**C.W.**	**Sp.**
2-3	Neutral	Rolled hem	Change foot & plate if necessary

- use a marker that you will be able to see on your fabric
- lightly 'dot' mark the fabric at 5cm (2 in) to 7.6cm (3 in) intervals along each side
- place a second mark 2.5cm (1 in) from the first
- ensure the intervals are regular, adjust as necessary
- mark clearly with removable marker
- cut 8 strips of Avalon™, each one longer than the fabric edge
- lightly 'dot' mark at 12.7cm (5 in) to 15.2cm (6 in) intervals

- place a second mark 2.5cm (1 in) from the first, adjusting as necessary to ensure they are even
- start serging your new edge finish along the Avalon™ strip
- at the 2.5cm (1 in) markers, stop
- lift the presser foot, place the Avalon™ strip and fabric together matching the 2.5cm (1 in) marks
- lower the presser foot, serge between the 2.5cm (1 in) marks
- the needle should just enter the outer edge of the previous row of stitching covering about ¼ of the stitch

please refer to photos

- chain off the fabric but remain on the Avalon™
- repeat the previous steps
- continue to chain off and on the fabric until the 4 edges are complete
- chain off on the last corner
- place a dot of Fray Stop on the ends of the thread chains closest to the fabric
- trim the excess chain once the sealant is completely dry
- gently tear the Avalon™ strips away if your fabric is not washable, or rinse in cold water and allow drying

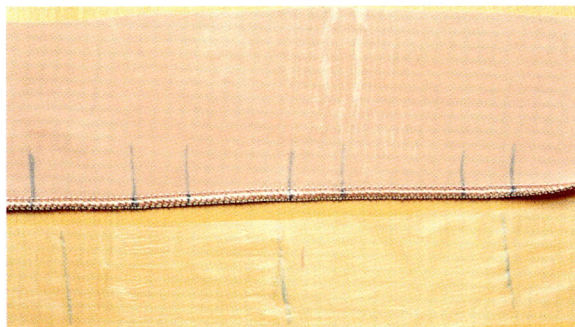

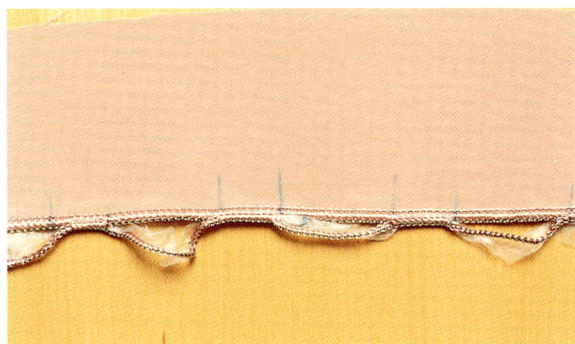

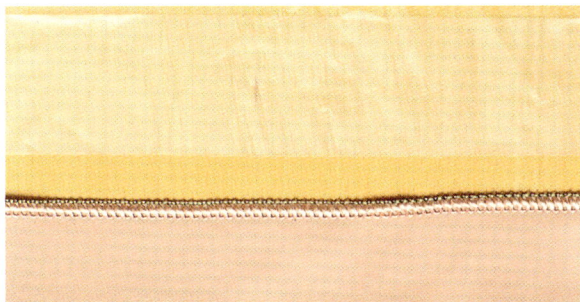

The Sumptuous Swag

the
sumptuous swag (cont)

Cornelli Couching

Setup

- thread the serger for a 3 thread rolled hem with Decor thread

3 thread rolled hem with decor thread

L.N.	R.N.	U.L.	L.L.
-----	Baseline	Looser	Tighten
S.L.	**D.F.**	**C.W.**	**Sp.**
2-3	Neutral	Rolled hem	Change foot & plate if necessary

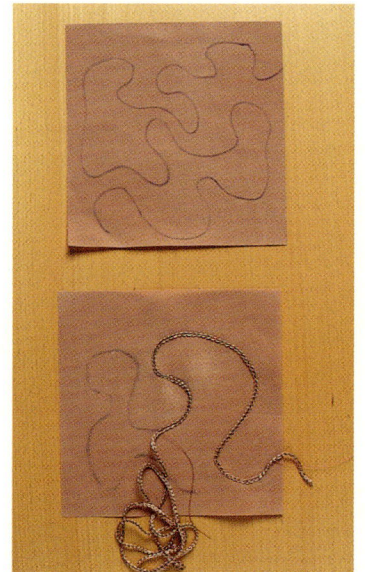

Method

- make serger chain by running the serger with no fabric under the presser foot. If it is not too even, serge over Avalon™ strips
- serge at least 5m (6¼yd) of chain
  – you can always make more if necessary

Retire the serger for the night after it has been cleaned and fed and continue with the sewing machine.

- thread the machine with the rayon, a matching Metrosene thread in the bobbin
- draw a simple but very loosely curved design in the corner of the shawl
- place dots of No More Pins along the design line
- gently press the serger made chain to follow the design lines

- place the open toe foot on the machine
- couch the Cornelli in place using a straight stitch, length 2-3
- further embellish the edges and the corner with lengths of chain tied to form voluptuous loops or tassles if you prefer
- hand sew crystals or beads to your liking
- brush or rinse out any markings, press

That's all there is to it. Legendary stuff. Time to make one more before the meal is done, eh?

aussie Christmas bush

Hi JF,

I really enjoyed your news the other day. No-one or nothing is meant to be that cold, surely? I can't imagine so much snow or a white Christmas. I'm shivering at the thought of it.

Christmas is about blistering heat, sun bleached skies, a trip to the beach, prawns and mangoes, a snooze after lunch. Not snow. Brrrr. Change of subject, that's giving me goosebumps.

I don't think I told you about our tree for this year, did I? We (me, I or all of us) seem to have misplaced things in the move. I can't honestly say that I miss the World's Best 5000 Schoolyard Jokes or that dreadful black nail polish (don't you you call it varnish?), but I became a bit frantic when the Christmas decorations couldn't be found. It's too far from town to bring a real / live Christmas tree and I can't find any of our native Christmas Bush which has fabulous green foliage and red flowers, around here. What's Santa's helper to do? Serge, of course.

Well, I went through the fabric scrap bag (the rest of the family are suspicious that none of the sewing supplies went 'missing') and found anything remotely red, green or white, or any of those combinations. I serged some decorative edges, made some bows and made my own 'Aussie Christmas Bush' with some sticks collected from the surrounding bush.

I'll send some photos and the 'recipe'. I think they are just soooooo simple and scrummy. What do you reckon ?

All the best for Christmas
Santa's Sergen' Helper

PS: Do you think Santa owns a serger?

aussie Christmas bush

Oh, for the simple things in life! Simple fabrics and sensational threads combine to create magic bows to trim an otherwise austere tree. They could just as equally be attached to a clip for a little girl's hair or to attach to the collar of the new puppy or kitten on Christmas morning.

Requirements

25 cm (¼yd)	4 different Christmas fabrics
Madeira	Decor # 1437-red
	Decor # 1479-green
Metrosene thread	2 reels red
	2 reels green

Universal # 80 needles

Craft Smart® Fray Stop

Spray starch or fabric finish

Rotary cutter, ruler and cutting mat

Avalon™ water soluble fabric

Instruction manual for your serger

Description

Fabric strips, with either a single or double row of embellishment

3 thread wide with decorative thread

L.N.	R.N.	U.L.	L.L.
Baseline	-----	Looser	Baseline
S.L.	D.F.	C.W.	Sp.
2½-3½	Neutral	Baseline	

3 thread narrow with decorative thread

L.N.	R.N.	U.L.	L.L.
-----	Baseline	Looser	Baseline
S.L.	D.F.	C.W.	Sp.
2-3	Neutral	Baseline	Change foot & plate if necessary

3 thread flatlock with decorative thread

L.N.	R.N.	U.L.	L.L.
Very loose	-----	Looser	Baseline
S.L.	D.F.	C.W.	Sp.*
2-3	Neutral	Baseline	Lower the cutting blade if preferrred

*See note in 'technical stuff'

3 thread rolled hem with decorative thread

L.N.	R.N.	U.L.	L.L.
-----	Baseline	Looser	Tighten
S.L.	D.F.	C.W.	Sp.
2-3	Neutral	Rolled hem	Change foot & plate if necessary

Method

The method for all the ribbon embellishment is very simple. The serger settings vary from your baseline with the introduction of a thick Decor thread always in the upper looper.

Simple Single Edging

- if the fabric is extremely soft, spray starch and press it
- thread the serger for the technique of your choice
- cut fabric strips selvedge to selvedge; cut selvedge off
- serge the long edges of each strip of fabric right side uppermost, chaining off the end of the fabric
- place a dot of Fray Stop on the ends of each of the thread chains closest to the fabric and a thin line across the raw fabric edge
- trim the excess chain once the sealant is completely dry

Simple Double Edging

- repeat the steps for single edging
- rethread your serger with a colour different to the original edging
- reset for a narrow finish or rolled hem
- using Avalon™ as a leader, serge your new edge finish. The needle should just enter the outer edge of the previous row of stitching overing about ¼ of the stitch
- place a dot of Fray Stop on the ends of each of the thread chains closest to the fabric and a thin line across the raw fabric edge
- trim the excess chain once the sealant is completely dry

Flatlocked accent (or 'hey diddle-diddle, lets flatlock in the middle)

Method #1

- thread the serger for 3 – thread flatlock
- cut fabric strips selvedge to selvedge; cut selvedge off
- serge the along the fold of each strip of fabric, right side uppermost, chaining off the end of the fabric
- place a dot of Fray Stop on the ends of each of the thread chains closest to the fabric and a thin line across the raw fabric edge
- trim the excess chain once the sealant is completely dry
- gently pull the fabrics apart

Method #2

- thread the serger for 3 – thread flatlock
- cut fabric strips selvedge to selvedge; cut selvedge off
- serge the along the edge of each strip of fabric, right side uppermost, chaining off the end of the fabric
- place a dot of Fray Stop on the ends of each of the thread chains closest to the fabric and a thin line across the raw fabric edge
- trim the excess chain once the sealant is completely dry
- finish the outer edge as you prefer

Make your ribbon strip into bows and 'bingo' that's it. Simple. It's Christmas

Hi JF,

I am so glad we moved here, I am enjoying this place more and more.The birds sound just wonderful in the morning and it is always fresh. I still have some pangs for the city, but not when I think of driving in the traffic or wall to wall people. I'd just like to be able to whip into town and get what I when I want it, instead of having to try remembering to write long lists.I end up with too much of some things ,not enough of others.Is that the first signs of a maturing brain? I suppose I'm still not completely 'countrified' yet.

Sometimes however , necessity is the mother of invention or something equally prosaic. I was playing at the serger and only had dark greys, blacks and some sparkly black thread. I started doing 'back flip sergery'. I think that is going to be a new serging term for me.

Anyway, I kept playing and ended up with all these strips of serger fabric. You know me, the world's neatest sewer: the strips had fallen to the floor and when I went to pick them up, I saw these burnt tree and charcoal images. I started to have a go at making a burned out tree stump.

When it all came together, I had it propped against a few pieces of the red and gold fabric from the Bushfire Quilt and Tamworth/Nashville shirt. It looked as though it was glowing, hence the Smouldering Log.

I'm really enjoying this form of sewing; 'Serger Art' if you like. I'll send the 'how-to' if you would like to try. Must go while I still remember

Bye for now

The Burnt Out Serger.

the smouldering log

the smouldering log

Glowing embers of gold and red encased in a seemingly innocuous black crust. The most dangerous element after a bushfire, the burned out trees fall to the ground, perhaps to spark anew, or hopefully to smoulder into oblivion. The Smouldering Log acts as a reminder of the awesome majesty of Mother Nature.

Requirements

Madeira	Decor # 1400	2 reels
	# 1441	1 reel
Madeira	Glamour # 2470	1 reel
Madeira	Rayon # 1000	2 reels at any one time
	# 1024	1 reel
	# 1107	2 reels

Universal # 80 needles

Avalon™ water soluble fabric in 30cm (12 in) x 2.5 (1 in) strips

Craft Smart® Fabric Stiffener, bowl, water, pastry brush

Rigid plastic tube

Craft wadding

Tie (binding wire) from a hardware store

Chicken wire

Re-cycled plastic shopping bags

2 chairs

Broom

50cm (½yd) red, gold, ochre fabrics (leftovers from The Bushfire Quilt or Tamworth to Nashville shirt)

Instruction manual for your serger

No, I haven't forgotten to put any quantities in the requirement list, but I would ask – how long is a piece of string? I cannot be more specific as I do not know if you are going to make a twig, a branch or an entire tree. Play and find out whether or not you like the technique first, before you commit more resources (or decide that I'm more than likely certifiable)

Description

Free form serger art work

Method

before you start

Do not try to become a Formula One racing driver with this project. Practice first before you increase your speed to ¾ of full throttle. Working with dark threads is challenging enough on its own without adding extra laps.

Setup

- thread your serger for 4 thread with Decor in the upper and lower loopers, rayon # 1000 in both needles

4 thread with Decor thread

Upper and Lower Looper

L.N.	R.N.	U.L.	L.L.
Baseline or a little looser	Baseline or a little looser	Looser	Looser
S.L.	D.F.	C.W.	Sp.
3-4	Neutral	Baseline	Reduce speed to 2/3

3 thread wide with rayon thread

L.N.	R.N.	U.L.	L.L.
Baseline	-----	Baseline	Baseline
S.L.	D.F.	C.W.	Sp.
2-3	Neutral	Baseline	Reduce speed to 2/3

Method

"Back flip sergery"

- thread the serger for a 4 thread with Decor in the upper and lower loopers
- serge on the Avalon™, the length of the strip, cutting a sliver off as you go
- run the chain off the end of the Avalon™ for 5cm (2 in)
- do not cut it, just flip it over-the back flip
- you can now serge from the chain end back towards the starting point
- the left needle should just enter the outer edge of the previous row of stitching covering about ¼ of the stitch
- "back flip" and go the other way, again serging over a strip of Avalon™
- continue in this manner until you have a piece of 'serger-made' log

the smouldering log (cont)

Adding the "mouldy" bits

- re-thread the serger for the 3 thread wide with rayon thread # 1024 in the upper looper, # 1107 in the needle and lower looper
- serge along the edge of the log 'fabric', starting about a ⅓ from the end
- the left needle should just enter the outer edge of the previous row of stitching covering about ¼ of the stitch
- serge to the middle of the log
- lift the presser foot and slide the stitches off the stitch finger
- 'back flip' and go the other way, again along the mouldy edge
- continue in this manner until you have a piece of serger made mould, around 3 or 4 rows
- thread the serger for a 4 thread with Decor in the upper and lower loopers
- resume the 'back flip' sergery, serging off the edge of the log just before the mould for a short distance
- serge on to the edge of the 'mould'
- the left needle should enter the outer edge of the previous row of stitching covering about ¼ of the stitch, along the upper edge of the 'mould'
- serge off the the edge of the 'mould' and join the main body of the log again

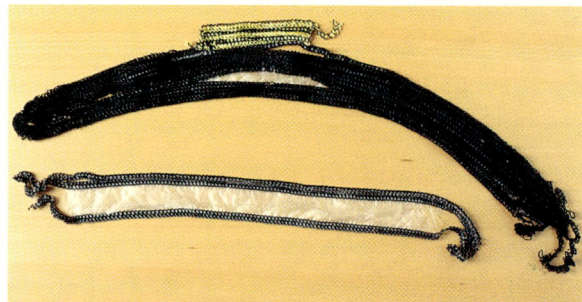

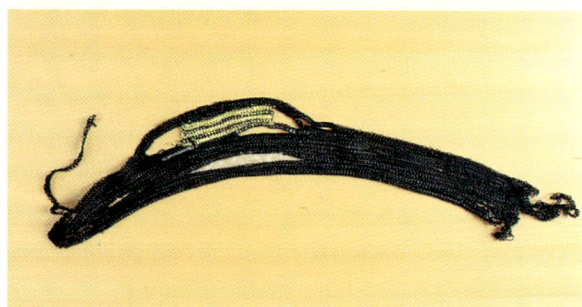

- as you gain confidence with the technique, start creating holes in the logs-this does not save thread but creates interest
- vary the thread colours for the log strips
- leave the serger chain ends attached unless you prefer the log to look freshly hewn
- join the strips into 1 flat piece, back-flipping them together

Construction

- choose a plastic tube that roughly conforms to the length of the log you have made
- wrap the tube loosely with craft wadding

- secure with plastic strips made from shopping bags
- cut a hole in the bottom of more plastic bags
- slide over the tube and wadding, telescoping them
- cover the wadding completely and secure with with more plastic strips
- rinse the log panel in cold water to remove excess Avalon™
- place the log panel over the prepared tube
- secure with tie / binding wire
- run the broom handle through the plastic tube *(ignore the jibes from the children about you adding an extra cylinder to your car)*
- support either end of the car (AKA broom) on the chairs
- place on a large piece of plastic or work above a surface that can be washed down
- in the bowl, prepare the Fabric Stiffener

- mix equal amounts of Fabric Stiffener and water
- using the pastry brush, apply the solution to the log, thoroughly saturating it

- allow to dry
- if necessary, apply another mixture of prepared solution
- remove the wire

You should now have a free form log with 'mouldy bits', holes, and lots of texture. Amazing isn't it? Let's add the 'S' to make it smoulder

- take the chicken wire and roughly shape it to the dimensions of the log
- cover with the fabric scraps and mold until the embers are formed
- position the embers in the log until you are satisfied with the effect

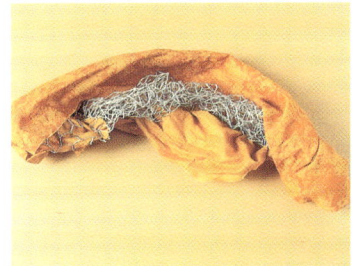

Get the children to clean up the mess; they're not allowed to play with fire

Hi JP,

As usual this letter is way overdue. I saw a sign the other day that changes the perspective, though. It read "you're so far behind, you're first." So this is not really overdue, you just haven't caught up yet. OK? My family reckons I'm going bonkers - they may just be right.

Anyway, I now have some self-imposed therapy. I'm making serger dollies. I had all these left over thread reels and being a bit of a collector, had them sitting around. We were having a big clean up and I had this inspirational flash (I know I'm heading that way but I don't think it was a hot flush) and pictured some dolls made on re-cycled reels.

You know how my brain goes feral sometimes - well it did it in a big way with these babes ! I decided right from the beginning that they were going to be worldly women and not naïve, giggling teenagers. They changed status as I made them, mainly due to a few slips of the pen when it came to drawing their faces.

These are Reel Blondes (because that is the only fabric and doll hair I had at home) and not one of them is called Marilyn. Why do I set myself challenges like this ? Am I really that stupid? Isn't that where you guys don't answer and invoke the 5th amendment on the grounds of incrimination? Anyhow, each one is a little different from the others because as each new generation was created they improved ,though maybe not in their opinion.

I'll send you the basic doll instructions, have a play and I know you'll do your own thing. Maybe we should have a Reel Dolls "meet" next time we are in the same country. Can't wait until I get some other hair colours during the next trip to town. Will they evolve into Reel Wild Women, Reel Worried Women, Tired Old Tarts. Think up a few names and we may have a quest for the best name - Terrific Older Teachers for starters?

Bye from
The Rumbustious Redhead

reel
blondes

reel blondes

Where do you start with a bunch of serger renegades like these 'Reel Blondes'? They do not have individual identities – I suppose Barbie® didn't either, she was never called June, Freda, Helga, Margot or Ethel. And she never had an attitude – or a figure – like these worldly women. Love'm or hate'm, they're here to stay. So there.

Requirements

Fabric: 15.2cm (6 in) x 7.6cm (3 in) scraps of whatever you think the girls would like for their dresses

12.7cm (5 in) x 12.7cm (5 in) squares for their heads – your choice of skin tone nylon netting

Thread: 2 reel ....Madeira Decor (to match fabric)

1 reel ....Madeira Rayon (to match fabric)

Universal # 80 needle

Avalon™ water soluble fabric

Empty Decor or Glamour reel/s

Craft wadding

Doll hair

Craft Smart® Tacky Craft Glue

8 amp fuse wire

Fine permanent marking pens, black and red

Description

Re-invented scraps – a serger 'scrappy' doll

As there is only one "Sergical Procedure" with these dolls, let's do it first

Setup

- thread the serger for a rolled hem with Decor thread

3 thread rolled hem with decor thread

L.N.	R.N.	U.L.	L.L.
-----	Baseline	Looser	Tighten
S.L.	D.F.	C.W.	Sp.
2-3	Neutral	Rolled hem	Change foot & plate if necessary

Method

- make serger chain by running the serger with no fabric under the presser foot. If the chain is not even, serge over Avalon™ strips
- serge at least 1.8m (2 yd) of chain-you can always make more if necessary-put aside
- using the same stitch, serge the net (no e-mail available yet) along the edges until you have lengths of at least 91.5cm (1 yd), put aside
- take the fuse wire and lay on the dress fabric
- serge slowly, the thread wrapping over the wire as you go along
- cut the wire just prior to chaining off

The Head

- place the fabric for the head on a table (not the operating one, we'd never ear the end of it)
- place a square of wadding in the centre of the square
- take 2 opposing corners and tie together
- repeat for the remaining corners
- wrap a long length of fuse wire firmly around the neck (no comment)
- slip the wire and fabric down the central canal of the empty reel
- ensure 5cm (2 in) to 7.6cm (3 in) of the wire protrude from the reel

The Arms.......

- take a length of serger chain and determine how long to make the arms
- close your eyes while you tie it around her neck-add a dab of glue just to be safe
- tie knots for the elbows (optional) and wrists

.........legs

- take a length of serger chain and determine how long to make the legs
- secure the legs at the bottom of the reel with the fuse wire
- tie knots for the knees and ankles

and Boomps-a-Daisy

- dab the reel with craft glue
- take a small strip of wadding
- wrap it around the 'body' of the reel for insulation against the rigours of life

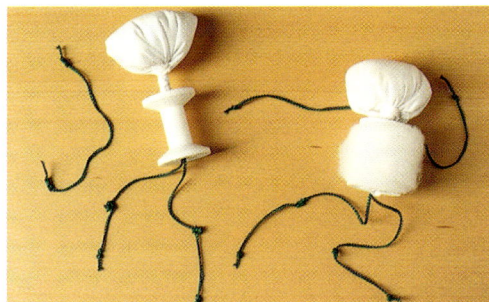

reel blondes (cont)

The Dress

- place the wire-edged dress over the reel
- cover the wadding and the junction of the neck and arms
- manipulate the dress until 'madam' looks right
- if there is any doubt about maintaining decorum, use craft glue to hold the frock in place

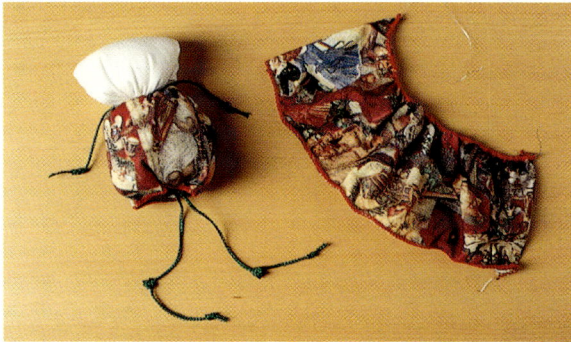

This reel doll was not meant to be bald-just take a look if you don't believe me

.....at the Hairdresser

- follow the instructions on the packet as to how to apply the crowning glory, using the craft glue as required
- make sure these girls have no thinning patches, they prefer Big Hair

........and at the accessories counter

- tie the bow and adorn the Reel Blonde as you wish- use some glue so there is no embarrass- ment in public places

The Attitude (aka the face)

This step requires some practice first if you want to get the attitude 'just so'. If you don't give her a face, you won't know what she is thinking..... that may be just as well if she's cranky. Other than that try what you will, this babe's just glad to have the chance to make her mark

.....and voila, you've got yourself a walking, talking, squeaking, squawking living doll

the bunyip cave

Well hello again

It's been pretty quiet around here with the troops away on holidays;it must be an army, the noise they make, the food they eat and the manouevres they pull.I suppose feeding the chooks (hens to you), dogs, cats and so on is the price I have to pay for being on my own. YAHOO!! I can sit and sew with no interruptions for dinner, homework supervision etc. - you know the drill.

A friend of mine has greatly relieved my mind - she strongly suggests that dust is the best furniture preservative known to sewers.There's this great thing about sewer's dust,it never gets any higher-when did you last find dust 6 inches deep? I was wondering if it was better to wait until it felted and instead of dusting and disturbing the air, you could lift it up in one entire piece. I can justify another hour a day at the machine now- as if I really have to !!

I was having a play at the serger the other day -OK,OK, another play-- I hadn't really explored the cover hem or chain stitch options on my serger but didn't have any clothes fabric and had to do something different. I'm not a rabid greenie, but some re-cycling appeals and I had loads of off-cuts from the Bushfire Quilt and Tamworth/Nashville shirt.

Anyway JF,this magic cavern is what evolved. I'm sure when you're going like you're on fire 'things' evolve rather than being created.Strange forces at work-maybe the thought of the troops getting back. Maybe a place our own mythical Bunyip would play in. Oh, a Bunyip is a bit like the Yeti or Abominable Snowman, and can be whatever you'd like it to be, I think. I don't know, I've never seen one. I only hope the cave is the right size.

I'm sure mine is a flamboyant Bunyip because of the colour in the cave - I hope so, I added lots of bits of glitz.What I'm really thrilled about is doing work on the serger which was 'traditionally' done on sewing machines. A new tradition perhaps ?? Why not?

Bye for now from
The Cavewoman

the bunyip cave

You can't do that on a serger! Have you heard that before? If we all lived by the rules perhaps we'd end up like the Bunyip, a creature of myth and legend. We would always wonder what we could have done if only we'd had the courage.

The Bunyip Cave explores the use of the cover stitch and the chain stitch in serger art. The sergers that offer this function can be quickly converted from their conventional stitching. There is also a dedicated serger available which performs only the cover and chain stitch. If your serger does not possess these features, don't despair. The body of the work can be done on a sewing machine, returning to the serger to complete the entrance and exit.

Requirements

Fabric scraps

Avalon™ water soluble fabric

Madeira	Monofilament 3 reels 1000m	clear
	optional: spool net covers	
Madeira	Rayon	# 2054
		# 1169
Madeira	Glamour	# 2414
		# 2465
		# 2425
		# 2424

Universal # 80 needles

Craft Smart' Fabric Stiffener, bowl, pastry brush

Balloons

Plastic pegs

Water soluble marker

Instruction manual for your serger

Description

Free form serger art work

the bunyip cave (cont)

Setup

- thread your serger with monofilament in both needles and the looper

Cover stitch with monofilament

L.N.	R.N.	LOOPER
Slightly looser	Slightly looser	Baseline
S.L.	D.F.	Sp.
3-4	Neutral	Spool net cover if required

- set up the serger for coverstitch; if you have the option on your serger, use the widest setting
- thread with monofilament in both needles and the looper
- apply spool net covers if preferred

Method

The Cave Walls

- cut the Avalon™ into 30cm (12 in) squares
- lay on a flat surface
- place fabric scraps or lengths of the Glamour threads on one side of the square
- fold in half, encasing the fabric
- place under the presser foot

- serge 3 or 4 pieces in a long row, joining the last piece to the first
- you have now formed a circle
- serge to your heart's content until the scraps of fabric hold together in their Avalon™ casing
- work on both sides of the strips to distribute the threads more evenly
- remove the circle of strips from the serger
- hold them up to the light or use a light box – a few holes are OK. Any more indiscretions and the cave wall will collapse
- serge and review until you have created your unique fabric
- join numerous fabric pieces until you have enough for your Bunyip to live in comfort
- put aside for the moment

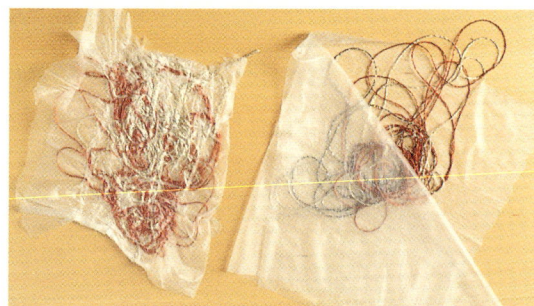

Setup

- set up your serger for the chain stitch
- thread the needle and looper with rayon thread

CHAIN STITCH

NEEDLE	LOOPER
Baseline	Baseline
S.L.	Sp
3-4	Spool net cover if required

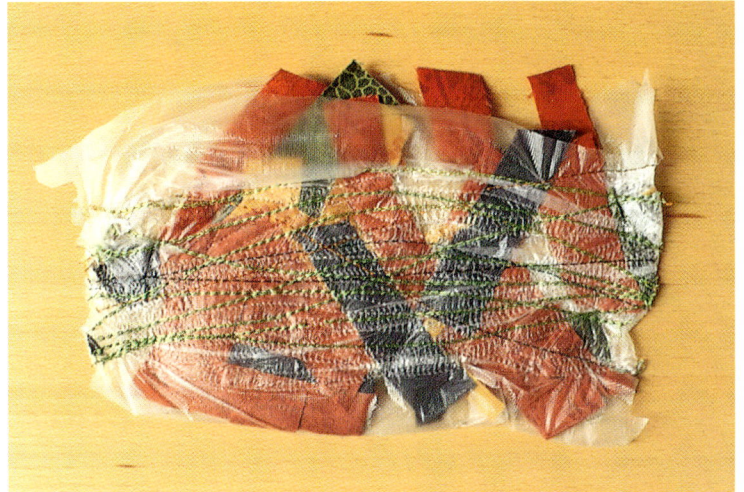

Method

- take your fabric for the Bunyip Cave
- place under the presser foot
- chain stitch all over the fabric
- periodically reverse the fabric as the needle thread and the chain stitch give quite different results
- remove from the serger when satisfied that your Bunyip will feel at home

You will now have a rather peculiar looking creation that in no manner, shape or form resembles a cave. It's flat. Time for the odd nip and tuck and the miracles of 'plastic sergery'.

the bunyip cave (cont)

Setup

- thread the serger with Glamour in the upper and lower loopers, either colour rayon thread in the needle

Plastic Sergery

Method

- inflate one or more of the balloons, tie securely
- take the fabric and roughly form it into a ball shape over the balloon(s)
- make varying size tucks, holding secure with plastic pegs
- mark the tucks with the water-soluble pen
- remove the pegs and balloon(s)
- match the pen markings, place fabric under presser foot
- serge 2 or 3 tucks only, on either side of your fabric piece

- start creating the edge of your cave
- serge the edge of the fabric
- at varying intervals, serge off the fabric leaving the length of chain intact
- resume serging on the fabric, creating your own nips and tucks as you go

Time to include some 'back flip sergery' to give more depth to the edge

Setup

- thread the serger for a 3 thread with Glamour in the upper and lower loopers

3 thread wide with glamour thread

L.N.	R.N.	U.L.	L.L.
Baseline	-----	Looser	Looser
S.L.	D.F.	C.W.	Sp.
2½-3½	Neutral	Baseline	Thread loopers using the dental floss threader

Method

- cut strips of Avalon™ 30cm (12 in) long
- serge on the Avalon™, the length of the strip
- cut a sliver off as you go, joining to the edge of the cave body
- run the chain off the end for 5cm (2 in)
- do not cut it, just flip it over – the back flip
- you can now serge from the chain end back towards the starting point
- the left needle should just enter the outer edge of the previous row of stitching covering about ¼ of the stitch
- "back flip" and go the other way, again serging over a strip of Avalon™

Let's make this cave a little more habitable.

Construction

- rinse the cave creation to remove the excess Avalon™
- in the bowl, prepare the Fabric Stiffener
- mix equal amounts of Fabric Stiffener and water
- inflate enough balloons to comfortably fit the cave
  - rest the balloon on a plastic sheet or an area that can be washed down
  - apply the solution to the cave, thoroughly saturating it
  - allow to dry
  - if necessary, repeat application of the solution
  - remove the balloons

You may now perform all of these procedures at your whim. The Bunyip will be amazed at your skill; just remember, however, that this sort of plastic sergery is not reversible.

Place in a convenient nook for your Bunyip to come and go as it pleases. There may be more out there, so it might be a good idea to start another cave.

Hi JF,
          Greetings from all of us to all of you. I've just re-
read that and realised it sounds a bit silly. I think the heat is
getting to me.
          I don't know whether we introduced you to the Great
Aussie Salute when you were over. I can hear you asking "What is
it ?" - a sorry disappointment actually - waving away 'blowies'
(blow flies). I don't know that there is any other country in the
world where the flies are so sociable and really are 'in your
face'; it requires a constant sweep of your hand like a
windscreen-wiper, to keep them away.
          I think I side tracked to this subject after a walk in
the bush at the back of the house. There were so few blossoms or
blooms .Gee that's a bit proper isn't it? No flowers,actually.
Lots of wonderful Aussie colours, greys, muted olive-greens,
subtle pink-browns etc., but no flowers. I really started thinking
how I could sort that out - the frosts kill so much and if they
had a plant equivalent to the RSPCA (yours is without the R
isn't it) I'd never be allowed to own anything, its my 'black
thumb' syndrome.
          What's a girl to do ? Sat down at the serger with this
on my mind and decided to work it out myself. Started finoogling.
I won't say it came in a blinding flash, took me a few kilometres
/ miles of thread before I finally created the Banksia Bouquet. I
worked with variegated threads which I have never been totally
satisfied with before. I think I had too much satin-stitch finish
which makes them look too chunky, but on the serger they have
just worked out deeeeeevine. I have not perfected the leaves yet,
but have the flowers fixed on to some thick real Banksia boughs.
I am delighted how they have worked out, the colours are either
very subtle or very strong. Hope you make up your own little
piece of the bush - will send some instructions.
          I think I may as well finish as silly as I started - I
hope this finds you as it leaves me.

          Bye from the Big Bad Banksia Woman

the **banksia bouquet**

the banksia bouquet

I cons of the Australian bush, Banksias have a majesty that sets them apart from other native plants. Stunning colours and varieties, they are found the length and breadth of the continent. The flower heads are surprisingly robust looking, yet on closer inspection they are both intricate and ethereal. Truly regal.

Requirements

Madeira Rayon ....3 x 200 m reels ....see separate table for
....colour combinations

Universal # 80 needles

Avalon® water soluble fabric in 30cm (10 in) strips

Craft Smart® Fray Stop

15.2cm (6 in) squares of nylon net to blend with thread colours

45 cm (½ yd) jumbo piping cord
(this is sufficient for 3 blooms)

Brown toned cold water dye, bucket, and gloves

Tie or binding wire from the hardware store

Instruction manual for your serger

Description

Floral serger art

Setup

- thread the serger for 3 thread with rayon thread

3 thread wide with rayon thread

L.N.	R.N.	U.L.	L.L.
Baseline	-----	Baseline	Baseline
S.L.	D.F.	C.W.	Sp.
2-3	Neutral	Baseline	Reduce speed to ⅔

Banksia colour combinations

Left Needle	Upper Looper	Lower Looper
1025	2023	1126
1024	2144	1126
1024	2053	1169
1078	2022	1024
1078	2145	1024

Method

The Flower Heads
"Back flip sergery"

- serge on the Avalon®, the length of the strip, cutting a sliver off as you go
- run the chain off the end of the Avalon™ for 5cm (2 in)
- do not cut the chain, just flip it over – the 'back flip'
- you can now serge from the chain end back towards the starting point
- the left needle should just enter the outer edge of the previous row of stitching covering about ¼ of the stitch
- 'back flip' and go the other way, again serging over a strip of Avalon™
- continue in this manner until you have a piece of serger-made Banksia flower
- leave the serger chain ends intact
- continue until you have made 1 flat fabric piece, about 15 cm (6 in)

- determine which side of the serger made fabric you prefer
- treating this as the right side, fold in half along the direction of the sewing
- serge carefully along the fabric strip
- the left needle should just enter the outer edge of the previous row of stitching covering about ¼ of the stitch
- chain off the fabric
- dot the chain ends with fray stop

- continue in this manner, serging the fabric edge at 1 cm (¼ in) intervals
- serge both remaining sides together to form a tube
- tuck the ragged thread chains to the inside at one end only

the banksia bouquet (cont)

- take the square of nylon net
- insert into the fabric tube, tucking the thread chains in at the same time
- rinse carefully but thoroughly to remove any Avalon™

The Stems

- wearing gloves, prepare the dye according to the instructions
- dye the jumbo piping cord keeping it firmly twisted
- allow to air dry
- unravel and separate into strands

- take the tie wire and make a bend in the middle
- wrap the strand of dyed cord along one side, then repeat for the other side

- create a gnarled, uneven stem

- shape the stem sufficiently to ensure that it remains stable when placed into the end of the Banksia

Attach directly to dense foliage or arrange in a display to showcase the regal heritage of these ancient plants.

About the Author

Anne has sewn most of her teenage and adult life, initially for pure "snob" value as she puts it: "The clothes I sewed looked equally as good, and as I got more experienced, even better, than anything I could buy. On student nurses' pay you had to stretch the money as far as possible. It didn't hurt the ego to look good and put your pay to having a good time- much more important in your 20's."

Marriage and children changed the body shape and the sewing direction, but never the passion. Working as a registered nurse after her first child was born, Anne found sewing for a child very satisfying and a safety valve from the pressures of combining motherhood and career. It was during her second pregnancy that Anne bought her first serger – and hated it. "I never had any proper instruction apart from a lighting talk about how to thread it. When I had the audacity to go back to the dealer and ask some questions about how to use it, I was shuffled out with the platitude that as an 'intelligent' woman, I shouldn't need any lessons. I sold it to a friend so that I could continue to enjoy sewing. I'm sure my daughter was a happier baby because of my actions."

When Anne started work as a consultant for a leading machine company she was confronted by a situation of total panic: to attend a trade show and demonstrate equipment. "I thought I would have to resign from what I considered the best job I'd ever had." She loved the machines but had an unnatural terror of the serger. Another consultant put it into perspective for her saying, "It's only a machine. It can't do anything wrong. Only the person sitting at it can." Her students have heard these wise words repeated at many of her classes.

A commitment to education has seen her become a sought after freelance teacher of both the serger and sewing machine, sewing the simple to the simply awesome. Surface embellishment has become her forum and has been expressed in such diverse forms as whimsical appliquéd dolls to 3D leaves and flowers: she is a contributor to some of Australia's leading magazines.

Join her on a discovery tour, Serging Australia: a truly pioneering journey into Overlocker Artistry.

Anne's e-mail address is:
dearanne@nepean.net.au

Sources & Suppliers

Threads & Aussie Publishers

AUSSIE PUBLISHERS
25 Izett Street Prahran Victoria 3181 Australia
Tel: 6 13 9529 4400 Fax: 6 13 9525 1172
Email: penguin@netspace.net.au
Website: http://www.penguin-threads.com.au

AUSTRALIAN PUBLICATIONS
3010 West Anderson Lane,
Suite G, Austin, Texas 78757
Tel: 1-888-788-6572   Fax: 512-452-3196
Email: sewmor@aol.com

MADEIRA AUSTRALIA
25 Izett Street, Prahran, Victoria 3181 Australia
Tel: +61 3 95294400   Fax: +61 3 95251172
Email: penguin@netspace.net.au

WALKER TEXTILE LTD
23 Fairfax Avenue, Penrose, Auckland, New Zealand
Tel: 0-9-579 0009   Fax: 0-9-579 5700

S.C.S. U.S.A.
9631 NE Colfax Street, Portland, Oregon 97220 U.S.A.
Tel: 800-547-8025/503-252-1452   Fax: 503-252-7280
Email: scs@madeirathreads.com

MADEIRA THREADS (UK) LIMITED
York Road, Thirsk, North Yorkshire, Y07 3BX, U.K.
Tel: 01845 524880 Fax: 01845 525046
Email: acts@madeira.co.uk

Patchwork Fabrics

DAYVIEW TEXTILES Pty. Ltd.
2/8-10 Deadman Road, Moorebank, N.S.W. 2170 Australia
Tel: +61 2 96008811   Fax: +61 2 96008899

RJR FASHION FABRICS
Tel: +1 310 217 9800   Fax: +1 310 217 9898

Heirloom Fabrics & Trims

HEIRLOOM ESSENTIALS
7 Bedford Road, North Epping, N.S.W. 2121 Australia
Tel: +61 2 98765484   Fax: +61 2 98768015

CAPITOL IMPORTS Inc.
P.O. Box 13002, Tallahassee, Florida 32317 U.S.A.
Tel: +1 904 385 4665   Fax: +1 904 386 3153

Craft Supplies

CraftSmart Australia Pty. Ltd.
43 Henderson Road, Clayton North, Victoria 3168 Australia
Tel: +61 3 95602042

Other books and videos by Aussie Publishers

Gary Clarke
- Embroidery and Candlewicking Designs
- Cats: Inspiration for Needlework
- Bouquets, Bows and Bugs
- Simply Flowers
- Candlewicking and Beyond

Stewart Merrett
- Appliqué Art
- Appliqué Alphabet
- Cross Stitch Pack

Jenny Haskins
- Amadeus
- Machine Embroidery, Inspirational Quilting Techniques

Judy Thomson
- Heirloom Timepiece

Videos

Jenny Haskins
- A Touch of Class – Sewing with Metallic Threads
- Over the Top – Decorative Overlocking/Serging

Leisa Pownall
- The A to Z of Hand Embroidery
- More Embroidery Stitches and Shadow Embroidery
- Animals & Flowers in Bullion Stitch
- The Wonderful World of Smocking

Eileen Campbell
- Machine Appliqué
- Basic Free Machine Embroidery
- An Introduction to Machine Quilting

Nola Fossey
- Creating Wearable Art

Gabriella Verstraeten
- Having Fun with Machine Embroidery
- Appliqué with a Difference

Styling & Props

Wedding Dress Quilt
Tiara from Wendy Louise Designs,
Ritz Carlton Promenade,
33 Cross St., Double Bay, N.S.W. 2028 Australia
Tel: +61 2 9362 0196

Glory Box Shirt
Silver brush, silver dish, glass bottles etc. from
Mosman Antique Centre,
700 Military Road, Mosman, N.S.W. 2088
Australia
Tel: +61 2 9968 1319

Thank-you

Like anything else in this book, the ideas may have been mine but without the appropriate requirements they would never have come to fruition.

Requirements

My husband, Phil – the childminder, the rapidly improving cook, part time typist and full time, never wavering, encourager and supporter

Our children, Dirk and Nina – the coffee-maker and kiss giver, who had a do-it-yourself school holiday and are growing into pretty good people but far too fast

Daryl and Michael – who gave me the opportunity on blind trust, the threads by the kilometre and no rules to break

Cheryl and Lisa – who listened to an idea and whose fabrics completed the picture

Andre and Kathy – the magicians of film and style who captured the spirit of the projects so aptly

Those who have been friends for a long time and loaned me their eyes and their fingers when mine refused to function – Ailsa, Karen, Janelle

Michelle for the critical appraisal of the quilt notes to ensure they really were understandable

Thank you all

Notes

Notes